Come, Find Space with God

Guidelines for Life Through Spiritual Practices

Leoma Gilley and Carol Mullen

Come, Find Space with God
Guidelines for Life through Spiritual Practices

The icon image used in Chapter 9 is used with permission.
Photo in Chapter 11 by Alison Crabb used with permission.
Edited and Proofed by First Editing
Cover and Interior Design by 100 Covers

Library of Congress Control Number: 2025928213
Names: Gilley, Leoma Gail, 1950-, author. | Mullen, Carol McConnell, 1962-, author.
Title: Come , find space with God : guidelines for life through spiritual practices / Leoma Gilley and Carol Mullen.
Description: Includes bibliographical references. | Knoxville, TN: AfNo Press, 2026.

Identifiers: ISBN: 978-0-9798966-8-2 (paperback)
978-0-9798966-9-9 (ebook)

Subjects: LCSH Spirituality. | God (Christianity) | Christian life. | BISAC RELIGION / Christian Living / Devotional Journal | RELIGION / Christian Living / Spiritual Growth
Classification: LCC BV4501.3 .G55 2026 | DDC 248.86--dc23

ISBN: (paperback) 978-0-9798966-8-2
eISBN: 978-0-9798966-9-9

Published by AfNo Press
820 Klondike Way, Knoxville, TN 37923
Email: thenomad@leomasbooks.com

For Ben, who helped me better understand the Gen-Z mindset.

Thank you for all the deep and honest discussions over dinner.

And with deep gratitude to Margaret Hill who enabled me to become free from my past and encouraged me to live out that freedom in the present.

The Order of St. Brigit, our spiritual community that has been such a blessing on our journeys.
And a special dedication to Susanne Vanzant Hassell, the founder of our order, who was devoted to creating and fostering our rich, contemplative community.
May she eternally be in the presence of the Lord.

Thanks to Steff Schneider, Mark Steimer, and Mike Ford for reading and commenting on the early draft.

Contents

Introductions

Life is challenging, especially as you become an adult with all the responsibilities that go with that. It can feel overwhelming, stressful, and very busy, which can result in anxiety, insecurity, and even fear. Most people feel they need some space or margin in their lives, but how do you find that? Jesus said, "Come to me, all of you who are weary and carry heavy burdens, and I will give you rest." (Matthew 11:28) This is a wonderful promise, but first, you need to recognize that you are overloaded and then come to Jesus. If you are willing to do that, this book is for you.

It helps to know where we are starting before we try to go somewhere else. So, after learning what's in this book and meeting the authors, we have a section for you to get to know yourself.

Each chapter includes stories, Scripture reflections, daily Scripture readings, music meditations, and spiritual practices that you can try. We expect each chapter will take at least a week, and possibly longer. You may use the books individually or as a group. Our goal is to provide a way to slow down, to draw closer to God, and grow as an active, mature disciple of Jesus.

You are encouraged to take time to write your reflections.

Leoma's Story

In 2017, Ben came to live with me. He was born and raised in Kenya, and when he entered the US, he was just sixteen, about to turn seventeen. Ben stayed with me for five years as he completed high school and studied mechanical engineering in college. As we shared many meals together, we had deep conversations about life, spirituality, God, purpose, life's challenges, racism, values, who we are, and why we are here on earth. As we are half a century apart in age, he wondered why I didn't have life figured out already so I could explain it to him.

As I spoke with more of my younger friends, I realized Ben was not the only one struggling with these questions. I remembered my twenties and thirties, and they were rough years. I made my worst mistakes during that period. So how could I use what I've learned over the years to guide my younger friends away from danger and toward being all God created them to be?

I'd recently had the opportunity to offer space for nine months while sharing my small home with a woman and her teenage son. During their stay, I found this quote:

"Hospitality is not to change people, but to offer them space where change can take place." [1]

I repeated it like a mantra when things got hard because I wanted to fix things, change their situation, but I couldn't. I had to remind myself I was just "offering them space." That led me to think about the need for us to find space with God to help us, change us, inspire us. Life is hard, and (spoiler alert) it doesn't get easier when we get older. In fact, moving from being a dependent child to a fully functioning adult is full of challenges. May God use this book to provide some guidelines for life to ease that process.

About This Book

No matter what stage of life you find yourself in, this book will provide a transformative experience as you find space with God. We feel it will be especially beneficial for people transitioning from living at home to living independently as adults. That's a time in life filled with wonderful opportunities, dangerous pitfalls, personal discovery, and lots of insecurity. How do we know? We've been there and have also watched our children go through the process. While this generation faces unique problems and challenges, there are helpful tools that can offer strategies and guidance. This is the opportunity for you to "find space with God" to make a difference.

Our goal is to ask questions that relate to your life, offer examples from Leoma's life, engage with Scripture, and provide spiritual practices that Christians have used for millennia. We have found them transformative, and we trust that you will as well. We want the scriptures to speak for themselves, so there are no long lectures. However, exploring the various practices and thoughtfully responding to the reflection questions are very important. Be honest with yourself and God—no one else needs to see what you have written. If you're in a group using these books, share only what you feel comfortable with. You are the primary beneficiary. Don't cheat yourself out of an amazing opportunity.

The chapters are designed to be used over the course of a week but take the time you need. If you take longer, it's not a problem. We offer Scripture readings for six days, assuming one day is for reading the book and engaging with the verses there. Find some time to do the spiritual practices suggested to see which ones work best for you. The playlist is available on this page.

Come, Find Space with God (https://subscribepage.io/LDTz9G)

Spiritual disciplines are *not* ways to get God to accept you or love you more. God already loves you more than you can understand. The practices offered here are simply a means to help you deepen your relationship with God and to learn to believe His promises. These "disciplines" are not rules—they are guideposts to a different way of living that is countercultural.

About the Authors

Leoma is originally from Chattanooga, Tennessee. As an only child in a neighborhood with no other children, she developed an active imagination and curiosity. However, nothing suggested the amazing life that awaited her. Much of her story is told in the Not How I Planned It memoir series. She lived as a single woman in the Sudan for over twenty years and has traveled widely throughout Africa and Europe. She has "borrowed" many African young people as her "children" and has learned so much from interactions with them.

Her adventures also led to exploring her inner life as well as the external one. She reflects deeply on the Scriptures and has found a deeper relationship with God, gaining a better understanding of the value of prayer. She is now a writer living in Knoxville, Tennessee.

www.leomasbooks.com

Email: thenomad@leomasbooks.com

Carol grew up in Ohio and spent ten years in South Florida after college before settling in Knoxville, Tennessee, where she has lived for twenty-eight years. She has two grown children and a new granddaughter. When she became an empty nester, she embraced her calling to train as a spiritual director. She completed three years of training, including a year focused on guiding directees through the Ignatian Spiritual Exercises. She also received certifications in both Life and Spiritual Coaching. For over ten years, Carol has been offering spiritual direction, workshops, and retreats—both in person and online.

Carol is a contemplative at heart and thrives in spaces where she can both receive and offer deep spiritual reflection and exploration. She provides a safe, sacred, deep listening space for her clients as they navigate their journey toward spiritual growth, freedom, wholeness, and a greater connection with God. www.soulssanctuaryspiritualdirection.com

About You, the Reader

Yes, the work begins here. Where are you in life? Let's begin by using Erikson's helpful categories and stages to assess.[2] We start with Stage 6 since this book is for adults. Where do you fit?

Life Stages

The following are Stages 6–8 of Erikson's psychosocial development theory, which focus on adulthood.

Stage 6 – Intimacy vs. Isolation (18-40 years): Love and intimacy in relationships with other people are very important during this time. If one is unsuccessful in finding a partner, they feel lonely and inferior. Romantic relationships are highly significant and vital for a nourished life, as are close friendships that provide closeness, honesty, friendship, and love. The virtue at this stage is love.

Stage 7 – Generativity vs. Stagnation (40-65 years): This stage is known as middle adulthood. Generativity refers to "making your mark" on the world through creating or nurturing things that will outlast the individual. It's a time to establish an ethnicity, a culture, a base that will guide the next generation. If you don't instigate change, then stagnation results. The virtue at this stage is care.

Stage 8 – Ego Integrity vs. Despair (65 years onward): During this time, people face internal conflict as they reflect upon their lives. Either they're satisfied with how things turned out, or they have a deep sense of regret. The virtue at this stage is wisdom.

✎ Take time to note where you find yourself.

Now let's consider your spiritual stage in life. Here are six stages, as defined in *The Critical Journey: Stages in the Life of Faith* [3]. Jesus calls us to be disciples, and as such, we must understand what a disciple is. In Jesus' time, teachers or rabbis chose the brightest and best to follow them, learn their teachings, and become teachers themselves. It wasn't a short, quick, one-and-done task—the disciples ate, drank, slept, lived, and worked with their rabbi.

Let's consider the stages of spiritual development to see how far we've come.

Stages of the Life of Faith

Stage 1 – Recognition of God

This marks the beginning of our faith and spiritual journey. We begin to recognize the presence of someone beyond ourselves who intersects with our lives. God's presence may be experienced through our senses, through a particular need in our life, or through moments of wonder and awe.

Stage 2 – Life of Discipleship

This stage is marked by learning about God through the instruction of others. It's an important part of our journey, as we learn of God through our teachers' instruction and live and grow in our intellectual knowledge of Him. We often develop a strong sense of right and wrong, but we may become stuck in black-or-white thinking or fall into an "us versus them" mindset.

Stage 3 – Productive Life

This stage is marked by active serving and leading within a church or faith community. For leadership roles, it is important to have a good foundation from the previous stage before moving into this stage. Stage 3 is a "doing" stage and can be accompanied by a sense of certainty and purpose.

Stage 4 – Journey Inward

Moving from Stage 3 to Stage 4 is often marked by a period of doubt, crisis, questioning, loneliness, and letting go of some of the productivity of the previous stage. This can feel unsettling as we navigate the mysterious inner journey God invited us into. It is often helpful to have a spiritual director accompany you as a co-discerner on your path toward growth and wholeness.

Many within faith communities never move beyond Stage 3 and are content to stay there. Stage 4 isn't a journey for the faint of heart, and it is often outside circumstances that propel us into it.

Stage 4B -The Wall

"The Wall" represents the moment when our will comes face to face with God's will. We decide anew whether we are willing to surrender and let God direct our lives. We may try everything we can to scale the wall, circumvent it, burrow under it, leap over it, or simply ignore it. But "The Wall" remains.

Psychological and spiritual healing often takes place in this stage. Each person's experience is unique—the Wall may come more than once in life and can last for varying lengths of time. Some remain stuck at the Wall and never move through it.

Stage 5 – Journey Outward

The outward journey is a venture outside our self-interests toward others, based on the growth and peace of mind we have experienced from the inward journey. This stage may or may not differ from our previous direction, but the focus changes.

Our focus is outward, but from a new, grounded center within ourselves.

Stage 6 – Life of Love

Stage 6 can best be described as a life that reflects God's presence and displays love and light in the world. The Spirit of God flows in and through us from day to day, often imperceptibly, and we are at work bringing God's Kingdom into our surroundings.

No matter where you find yourself, the exercises in this book can help you deepen your relationship with God. As you come to understand God's Word more deeply and learn to listen to what He is saying through it and other means, you will become more confident in your decisions and life choices. There is nothing like having the all-knowing creator of the universe as your guide through life.

"It's at the heart of everything we struggle with in life: longing to be valuable, to be accepted, to be prized, to be worth something to somebody, to have a life that matters, and God's saying 'You matter! I didn't make anyone else like you. You're not a reprint or a lithograph. You're a one-of-a-kind, original creation of God.'" (Louie Giglio)[4]

✎ Take time to note where you find yourself spiritually.

____

____

____

____

____

CHAPTER 1

Be Still: Allowing God In

Who are the most important people in your life? Why? Are there other people you admire and want to be like? Who are they? Why do you look up to them?

____

____

____

____

____

Leoma's Story

After several years in Sudan, during my mid-thirties, I moved to England to "read for a PhD." My goal was to create a usable writing system for a language group in southern Sudan. Although I had training for this job, the language was defeating me, and I desperately needed more help to accomplish my assignment. On top of that, I had been living in a war zone in southern Sudan, which only added to my stress level.

I moved to a country that I mistook for one like the United States. Instead, I encountered very different ways of thinking and coping (for example, the belief that a cup of tea will solve any problem). I spent hours on buses, unsure where I was or when to get off. As soon as I opened my mouth, I felt "classed" because of my American accent—Americans are at the bottom of England's social ladder. In addition, it was cold and damp, and it was dark by 4:00 in the winter. Studying for a PhD was a stretching experience as well, and all these factors combined with the stress of living in southern Sudan during a civil war threatened to push me over the edge. I decided I needed counseling before something very serious happened.

A counselor I had met in the U.S. years before now practiced in England. But his approach had changed, and I found this new method didn't help. I became increasingly desperate for a solution, and at the peak of my crisis, he went on vacation.

In panic mode, I confided in my new friend, Margaret. After listening to my tale of woe, she asked if I would consider some prayer counseling sessions with her. I was so desperate at this point that I would have agreed if she had asked to hit me over the head with a hammer! Together, we created space for God to walk with me through the traumas of my life. Some seemingly insignificant incidents came to mind, yet when I revisited those with Jesus and Margaret, powerful emotions were unleashed. One such instance was when my first-grade teacher shamed me in front of the class for writing my letters "the wrong way" before she had instructed me. And why would that trigger a meltdown? Her messages had taken hold: *Don't be creative. Don't take initiative. You'll only mess it up, and everyone will know. Wait for someone to tell you how to do something because you're not clever enough to figure it out.* That message stuck with me for thirty years. But now Jesus was telling me differently: *Your teacher was wrong to say that. I want you to be courageous, strong, and creative. You can do anything if you follow me.*

As we worked through many past incidents, I felt lighter, brighter. In fact, as I walked across campus, I even skipped and danced. By the time my counselor returned, I didn't need him anymore. For the first time, I could express my anger, disappointment, and at times, fury, knowing that Jesus and Margaret were okay with me doing that.

Jesus continued to assure me that he is always with me and loves me no matter what. Finally, I gave God the space in my life that he needed to truly set me free. I can say "no." I can mess up. I can ask for help. The unhealthy coping strategies I had used for most of my life were no longer needed. I had found the One who loved me completely. All God asked was that I make space for him to do his work in me and through me.

What followed were a series of encounters with God in my interior world, a place I went when trying to figure out life. Jesus met me there as a young child, playing by myself inside a shed. He invited me to come out with him. I was hesitant, but eventually I agreed, and he led me into a nearby meadow. Unlike my dark and dusty shed, the meadow was a brilliant green, with wildflowers growing all around. There, I became a lamb, frolicking and tasting the delicious grass and flowers under the blue sky and warm sun. Then Jesus sat down in the middle of the meadow and invited me to sit on his lap. I snuggled into his arms, and we stayed like that for quite a long time.

But my old fears surfaced. *What if I moved? What if I ran away? Would he abandon me?* I had to know, so I got up and ran a few feet away. Then I looked back to see his reaction. Jesus was watching me, and he was smiling. I ran a bit farther and looked back. Jesus got to his feet, still smiling, and then playfully chased me. We raced around the meadow until I grew tired of the game. Jesus never "caught" me, though he could have. He sat down, and once again, I nestled in his lap. I had never felt so loved, so at peace.

Now and then, I looked back at the shed. I realized that it had caused me great pain and loneliness. I didn't want to go back there ever again.

And Jesus said, "It's time to leave this painful place. Come with me." He showed me a path that led through the meadow and up into the mountains.

"There?" I asked.

"Yes. You need to leave this place of pain and sadness. Come with me, and I will show you wonderful things."

And so I did.

Months later when he saw me looking down at the shed, the Shepherd said, "Don't worry, Little One. It's part of your past, but not of your present or future. The longer you are away from it, the less it will affect you. Come, let's continue our adventure."

And we have.

Engaging with Scripture

Psalm 23

1 The LORD is my shepherd;
I have all that I need.
2 He lets me rest in green meadows;
he leads me beside peaceful streams.

3 He renews my strength.
He guides me along right paths,
bringing honor to his name.

4 Even when I walk through the darkest valley,
I will not be afraid, for you are close beside me.
Your rod and your staff
protect and comfort me.

5 You prepare a feast for me
in the presence of my enemies.
You honor me by anointing
my head with oil.
My cup overflows with blessings.

6 Surely your goodness and unfailing love will pursue me
all the days of my life, and I will live
in the house of the LORD forever.

Psalm 23 As We Often Live It

1 The LORD is my backup plan
for when I have an emergency.

2 In the meantime, I race through
life at breakneck speed,
trying not to miss anything.

3 I get tired and depressed,
but I keep going on my chosen way
in hopes of bringing honor to my name.

4 When I walk through dark valleys
I ask "Why me? I don't deserve this!"
When I'm afraid, I ask
"Why did you let me get to this point?
Why don't you protect and comfort me?"

5 I feel fearful and helpless
in the presence of my enemies.
"Why don't they recognize my value and worth?
Why aren't my successes satisfying?"

6 Surely goodness and reward
will come to me
if I keep working hard enough.
And then I can rest
on my accomplishments
for the rest of my days.

Reflection Questions

Reflect on which version of Psalm 23 best represents your thoughts and attitudes.

Write down your responses.

- First, what is the role of the LORD in your life? Is he the leader or the backup plan?

- We have a choice about who controls our life—either we do, or we allow God to be in control. What guides your choice? And what are the possible outcomes of that choice?

- What does God offer?

- Are you ready to become a disciple of Jesus?

According to recent surveys, over 63 percent of the population in the U.S. identifies as "Christian." The same study identified the number of serious Christians as 4 percent. But what does that really mean? When Jesus invited Peter, James, John, and the others to join him, he didn't have them pray a prayer and then go about their lives. His instruction to his apprentices was "Follow Me." And that's what they did. They walked, listened, talked, and lived with Jesus for three years. They became "disciples" or "apprentices" to become like Jesus and live as he did. Are you one who mentally agrees to the doctrines that Jesus is part of the Trinity, that he came to die for our sins, and that if we accept his offer of salvation we are "saved"? Or do you long to become—or are you becoming—a true disciple, an apprentice of Jesus? [5]

If you are or want to become a disciple of Jesus, then the practices in this book can help you realize that goal.

Scripture Meditation

This week in your daily scripture readings, open yourself to seeing and experiencing what the Good Shepherd has to offer. What would it be like for you to trust Jesus with your life?

Reflect on the scriptures suggested for each day.

✎Be sure to write your reflections.

Day 1: **Psalm 139** Why would God have a better idea of how to live life than we would?

____

____

____

____

____

Day 2: **Jeremiah 29:11-14** What plans does God have for us?

____

____

Day 3: **Jeremiah 6:16-19** What if we reject God's way?

Day 4: **Romans 3:21-28** How can we find God?

Day 5: **John 3:16-21** How has God made a way for us to reach him?

Day 6: **Psalm 146** What does God promise those who trust him?

+ Spiritual Practices

As you reflect on the above verses, notice God's invitation to stillness and openness. The following practices will help you create space to welcome his presence.

Practice 1: Opening The Door of Your Heart to Jesus

Revelation 3:20

"Look! I stand at the door and knock. If you hear my voice and open the door, I will come in, and we will share a meal together as friends."

Take a close look at this familiar image of Jesus knocking on the door by Warner Salman[6]. What do you notice? Is there anything unusual about the door? Notice there is no handle on the outside, only the inside. What would your heart door look like? Are there locks on it? If so, what might they represent? What does Jesus's knock sound like? What does His voice sound like? What might prevent you from hearing his knock or his voice?

____

____

____

____

____

John 10:3-5

"The gatekeeper opens the gate for him. He calls his own sheep by name and leads them out. After he has gathered his own flock, he walks ahead of them, and they follow him because they know his voice. They won't follow a stranger; they will run from him because they don't know his voice."

1 Kings 19:11-12

"Go out and stand before me on the mountain," the Lord told him. And as Elijah stood there the Lord passed by, and a mighty windstorm hit the mountain. It was such a terrible blast that the rocks were torn loose, but the Lord was not in the wind. After the wind there was an earthquake, but the Lord was not in the earthquake. And after the earthquake there was a fire, but the Lord was not in the fire. And after the fire there was the sound of a gentle whisper. When Elijah heard it, he wrapped his face in his cloak and went out and stood at the entrance of the cave. And a voice said, "What are you doing here, Elijah?"

Our lives can become so busy that we miss the Divine Knock at the door of our hearts. During the coming week, try to find some moments of silence and solitude to listen for the voice of your Good Shepherd calling you by name. If you listen carefully enough, you might hear a question from God—or perhaps hear him answering one of your questions. The question Elijah heard was, "What are you doing here, Elijah?"

Now sit in stillness and allow God to ask you that question. "What are you doing here, [your name]?" Listen to how your heart responds to God.

✎ Be sure to record your reflections.

____

____

____

____

____

Prayer

"Opener of Hearts, you are the true guide of my life helping me unlock every door that leads to you. As I move amid the mystery of myself, I seek to know your desires for my growth. Keep showing me the way to you as I turn to you with trust and with faith. I open the door of my heart to you. I open the door."

—Joyce Rupp[7]

Practice 2: Offering Our Imagination to God

In this chapter, Leoma shared how she experienced healing, freedom, and wholeness by opening to Jesus through Imaginative Healing Prayer, which then opened her to a deeper connection with Jesus. If we have experienced any form of trauma in our lives, we may remain stuck spiritually until we offer space for Jesus to enter our pain through imaginative prayer. We may know scripture about God's care, love, and protection, but our body, mind, and soul won't register it as real. It isn't what we intellectually believe is true. In his book, *Seeing is Believing*, Boyd says, "it's what we experience as real ... a person can believe Christianity is true, but it will affect his or her life only to the extent that it is experienced as real."[8]

In the Middle Ages, St. Ignatius developed the Spiritual Exercises to help people grow spiritually. There were several prayer practices that enabled this growth, including Imaginative Prayer, which could be used with a Bible passage, as a discernment for the future, or to heal a memory of the past.[9]

It is amazing to witness the transformative effect that Imaginative Prayer, through the guidance of the Holy Spirit, can have on people's lives.

I invite you to experience Psalm 23 from this week's scripture readings imaginatively. Read it aloud several times, perhaps in a different translation than you're used to. Close your eyes and visualize the scene as if you're in a movie. Pay attention to the sights, sounds, tastes, smells, and feelings you might experience. Let yourself become part of the scene and the story.

✎ Journal about what you experienced in that exercise.

Practice 3: Offering Space to Another

- Think of someone who helped you when you were in need. If you're still in touch with them, drop them a note to let them know they are remembered and appreciated.

- Consider the people around you who may need a word of encouragement. Seek them out and show them God's kindness and love.

♫ Music Meditation

"*Still Waters*" by Leanna Crawford is suggested as a possible way to continue your meditation as you go into the world. Listen to what speaks to you from the playlist on the *Come, Find Space with God* page. Listening to it several times this week.

? Questions for Reflection and Discussion

1. Think back on a time in your own life when God came to you and helped you as your Good Shepherd or Good Samaritan. Write down your experience and consider sharing this God story with your discussion group.

    ____

    ____

    ____

    ____

    ____

2. Have you experienced a traumatic event from the past that is keeping you stuck on your spiritual journey? These experiences become attached to false beliefs and dysfunctional behaviors that hold us back from becoming the beloved children God created us to be. Take some time to reflect on one or two false beliefs or behavioral patterns attached to a past event that you need freedom from. Take these to God in prayer and journal. Consider receiving healing prayer from a trained practitioner. If you are comfortable, share with your discussion group some false beliefs or behaviors attached to them.

    ____

    ____

    ____

    ____

    ____

3. Was there a spiritual practice, scripture meditation, or reflection in this chapter that felt particularly important or resonated with you? Why? How did it affect your daily experience and finding space with God?

____

____

____

____

____

CHAPTER 2

Scripture: A Key to Transformation

We all come from different backgrounds and therefore have different expectations of how the spiritual relates to us. Perhaps you come as an atheist or from a faith unrelated to Christianity. How committed were your relatives to their beliefs? If your parent brought you up in a Christian tradition, is that tradition meaningful to you today? If so, in what ways? And if not, why not? Have you ever felt let down by your family—or even by God?

Spending time in the Scriptures can transform us. Let's discover how.

Leoma's Story

I was raised in a Christian home. My mother's faith was strong, but my father claimed to be an agnostic. In my early years, Mom and I were there when the church doors opened. As part of my training, I was instructed to read the Bible every day. When I entered college, I let that practice slip. But, in my mid-twenties, I made a deliberate vow to read the Bible every day for a year. Some days it came easily. On others, I managed only a few verses late at night before falling into bed. I may not have fully absorbed what I read, but it helped me form a lasting habit.

Over the years, I've participated in multiple Bible studies, both individually and in a group. Through those studies, I learned to pay attention not only to the message but also the theology. My understanding of God and of biblical history increased, and I saw how people either obeyed—or didn't obey—God's commands.

After many years, I had acquired a great deal of knowledge about the Bible.

But knowledge by itself wasn't enough. I grew tired of studies that focused on surface details—who did this or why that happened. It reminded me of the little boy in Sunday School who, when asked what he saw outside, replied, *"It looks like a squirrel, but it must be Jesus."* As one evangelist said, *"You know more now than you're living up to."* At some point, we master those surface things, but our spirits cry out for something more.

I wanted to hear God speaking to me. As God would have it, I was introduced to the contemplative practice of *lectio divina*—divine reading. At first, it felt like just another exercise. But when I complained to God that I wanted him to speak, he replied, "*Why don't you listen*?" Ouch.

As I began listening for a word or phrase in the passage I had chosen each day, I often didn't understand why that phrase struck me. In the second reflection, I asked, *"Why this word here? Why now?"* As the reason came to me, I moved to the next reading, engaging with God about it. Sometimes it pointed me to a fear I had, a personal relationship that needed attention, or simply a question I had for God. This is where I had to listen and take time to discuss things with Him.

When practiced in a group, where all of us are listening to the same passage, the discussion brings out many viewpoints and can be very insightful. Having hashed out the message God is trying to convey; I just rest and consider what I learned.

God has a great deal to say to us—but we need to listen. Reading and rereading a few verses can help us slow down and receive the hope, love, and comfort that we need in that moment. I've felt a closeness to God like never before, and it has changed my life.

Engaging with Scripture

In the *Life with God Bible*, Richard Foster says, "Reading, studying, memorizing and meditating upon scripture has always been the foundation of Christian Disciplines."[10]

"All Scripture is God-breathed (given by divine inspiration) and is profitable for instruction, for conviction (of sin), for correction (of error and restoration to obedience), for training in righteousness (learning to live in conformity to God's will, both publicly and privately-behaving honorably with personal integrity and moral courage); so that the (*people*[1]) of God may be complete and proficient, outfitted and thoroughly equipped for every good work."

(2 Timothy 3:16-17 AMP)

Lectio Divina is a slow, prayerful way of reading Scripture. Begin by coming prayerfully to your reading, asking the Holy Spirit to guide you to what is most relevant for your life right now. You may access the playlist on the *Come, Find Space with God* page to listen to the passage. Pause after each of the four readings and follow the prompts provided.

Lectio (reading)

Meditatio (reflecting)

Oratio (praying)

Contemplatio (resting)

I tend to avoid things that make me uncomfortable or that I disagree with. Can you relate to that? It's not surprising, then, that we might prefer to think that some of the Bible is not relevant or useful. Yet Paul challenges Timothy—and us—to recognize ***all*** of the Scriptures.

---

1 Inclusive language added.

Our culture and our world are broken by sin, so we can't rely on what is around us to be true. However, God's Word is true. It teaches us where we need to change and shows us where we are going wrong. None of us likes to admit we're "wrong," but we often don't see how far our standards vary from God's.

+ Spiritual Practices

During your scripture readings for this chapter, try these two ways of reading the Bible, recognizing that your engagement with scripture is more about **transformation** than **information.**

Basic Bible Study

Take one or two scripture passages and apply a basic four-step study method.

1. Observation: Examine the text to notice details and context such as characters, settings, and key message.
2. Interpretation: First, write your own interpretation based on your observations. Then you can use tools such as Bible commentaries or dictionaries.
3. Connection: How does this passage connect with your life?
4. Application: Consider ways you could apply the passage to areas of your life. Ask God for the grace to actively live out what you noticed.

Lectio Divina—Sacred Reading

Lectio Divina is an ancient practice of reading a passage of Scripture or a sacred text to experience not just head knowledge but spiritual transformation. The process is slow, meditative, and prayerful. Often, you choose a small portion of Scripture to reflect on deeply.

I have found *Lectio Divina* to be a life-giving, relevant practice for many years—both individually and within groups. Hebrews 4:12 reminds us that "scripture is living and active." Even when meditating on a familiar passage with *Lectio Divina*, I discover new revelations for where I am in my life. Using the practice within groups, such as the one I'm in with Leoma, has been a rich and expansive experience because of the variety of perspectives brought forth in our sharing creating a deeper, fuller meaning to the passage.

Come to your time with *lectio* prayerfully and expectantly, asking the Holy Spirit to guide you to what is relevant for your life right now.

There are classically four movements to this sacred reading:

1. *Lectio*: A slow reading of the passage, preferably aloud, for content. Listen for a word of phrase that calls to you, captures your attention.
2. *Meditatio*: Slowly reflect on your word or phrase allowing space for deeper revelation. Spend some time allowing it to speak more fully to you.
3. *Oratio*: Have a prayerful conversation with God based on your reflections. How does this word, phrase, or passage apply to your life? Listen for His guidance.
4. *Contemplatio*: Rest quietly in God's presence.

Contemplatio is an important but often forgotten portion of this practice. Rest quietly in God's presence. Release thoughts and be still.

✎ It's helpful to journal your experience. Write down your word/phrase. Then after your meditation, write what God is asking of you. As you complete your conversation with God, express what insights you have gained.

There is also an app for this practice called Hallow.

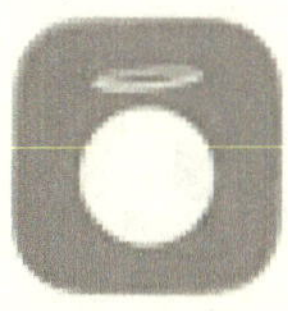

Scripture Meditation

Use one of the methods described as you read your passage for the day.

Day 1: **Psalm 119:33-40**

Day 2: **Isaiah 40:25-31**

Day 3: **Job 38**

Day 4: **Job 42:1-6**

Day 5: **Matthew 4:1-11**

Day 6: **Hebrews 4:12-16**

Music Meditation

Several songs are suggested for continuing your meditation as you go into the world:

Thy Word by Amy Grant, *Ancient Words* by Michael W. Smith, and *Show Me the Way, Lord* by Divine Tunes.

Listen to what speaks to you. You may choose a song from the playlist that resonates with you the most and listen to it several times this week.

? Questions for Reflection and Discussion

1. Was there a time in your life when your efforts to engage with God seemed dry and lifeless—when your spirit cried out for more? Perhaps those practices were once beneficial, but maybe the Holy Spirit was inviting you into something new through your inner longings. Did you discover new spiritual practices, or did you struggle for a while? Sometimes such struggles draw you closer to God, but sometimes they can push you farther away. If you're a new believer, it can be an exciting time of discovery where everything is fresh. Journal your experience.

____

____

2. As Leoma practiced *Lectio Divina* and listened to God, she discovered that the Bible really is relevant for her life. What are some areas of your life that might benefit from the Spirit of God guiding you through this form of Scripture meditation and conversation with God? Are there questions you would like to ask Him?

____

____

____

____

____

3. Was there a spiritual practice, Scripture meditation, or reflection in this chapter that felt particularly important or resonated with you from your time? Why? How did it affect your daily experience and finding space with God?

____

____

____

____

____

CHAPTER 3

Prayer: Deepening a Relationship with God

Even when we're around a lot of people, many of us still feel isolated and alone. Much of today's conversation takes place on social media, and we know from hard experience that sharing can sometimes be dangerous. People don't "get us," or they don't really care, so they write hurtful responses. It's hard to know who to trust with our concerns, questions, and fears. So where do you turn when life is hard?

Leoma's Story

When I was a child, my mother taught me a prayer:

God is great. God is good.
Let us thank Him for our food.
By His hands, we all are fed.
Thank you for this daily bread. Amen.

That prayer gave me the words to begin talking with God, but I remember wanting to express my own thoughts in prayer. But I was afraid I wouldn't do it right, so it took a long time to take the plunge.

For as long as I can remember, my mother took me to Wednesday night prayer meetings. It was a small but faithful crowd in our little country church. People would share concerns for us to pray over, and anyone was welcome to join in. If requests were sensitive, someone might say, "I have a silent request." I always dreaded the moment when one man prayed—he went on for what seemed like hours. From those meetings, I learned that prayer was important, but for many years, I understood it mainly as asking God for things. In my mind—and the minds of many, I suspect—God was like an ATM. Put in your identification, state what you want, and out it comes. Another picture I carried in my mind was of God as a bank manager from whom we asked a loan— "God, if you will do this for me, I'll do that for you. Is it a deal?"

Only later in life did I learn what prayer is supposed to be—a relationship with God rather than a transaction. God made an enormous sacrifice to bring us into a relationship with Him. This is why, when Jesus taught his disciples to pray, the first line was, "Our Father, who is in heaven." We are greeting our good father, acknowledging him and his role in our lives. Yes, there's a time and place for asking, but most of us have plenty of experience with that type of prayer. What we need most is to remind ourselves of our relationship with God.

When you think about prayer, what image or thought comes to mind? Journal your own definition of prayer.

Take a few moments to reflect and write about your experience so far on your journey with prayer. Why do you pray? Observe your experience without judgment.

Engaging with Scripture

9 Our Beloved Father, dwelling in the heavenly realms, may the
glory of your name be the center on which our lives turn. 10
Manifest your kingdom realm and cause your every purpose to

be fulfilled on earth, just as it is in heaven. [11] We acknowledge you as our Provider of all we need each day. [12] Forgive us the wrongs we have done as we ourselves release forgiveness to those who have wronged us. [13] Rescue us every time we face tribulation and set us free from evil. For you are the King who rules with power and glory forever. Amen.

Matthew 6:9-13 TPT

Reflection Questions

- What part of this prayer is most meaningful to you, and why?

____
____
____
____
____

- What are the different parts of the prayer?

____
____
____
____
____

- Should we simply repeat these words, or use them as a model to follow when talking with our Father God?

____
____
____
____
____

- Would you feel safe praying in this way? Why or why not?

____
____
____
____
____

✎ You might also try writing a prayer for yourself following this model.

____
____
____
____
____

Carol's Story

As a spiritual director, I listen as my clients describe where they are on their journey and discern with them what the Holy Spirit might be inviting them into during this season of life. No matter what form of prayer you feel drawn to, I would say the first step—and the greatest challenge—is **to offer space for God in both our physical and inner spaces.** Prayer is foundationally relational, and like any good relationship, it involves both speaking and listening. The practice of listening can take time to grow into. Many people think of prayer only as talking *to* God or *at* God.

Four Stages of Prayer

Thibodeaux [11] speaks of growth in prayer as happening in four stages, even though these types of prayer may be used at various times in our journey:

1. **Talking *to* God** – using written or memorized prayers such as *Our Father* or *Now I lay me down to sleep.*

2. **Talking *with* God** – continuing to use written prayers while also speaking to God with your own words and feelings.
3. **Listening to God** – entering into dialogue where we both speak and listen to God's subtle language of love.
4. **Being with God** – reaching a deep relationship where we are content to sit and rest in God's presence.

Ultimately, prayer should be real. We don't need to clean ourselves up and be perfect to come to God in prayer. Many people hold a false belief about prayer that hinders their intimacy with God, who calls us Beloved. As we open ourselves to God's presence, we are slowly transformed.

✎ When you think about prayer, what image or thought comes to mind? Journal your own definition of prayer.

____

____

____

____

____

Which of these stages reflects your prayers right now?

____

____

____

____

____

♥ Scripture Meditation

You may use these verses for your weekly reading. Consider the questions and write your responses.

Day 1: **Psalm 46** What do you learn about God in this Psalm?

____

____

____

Day 2: **Matthew 11:25-29** What is Jesus' offer to you?

Day 3: **Ephesians 4:1-18** How does God equip you to be the person he created you to be?

Day 4: **Philippians 3:12-16** Does God expect perfection?

Day 5: **Ephesians 2:4-10** How does God view you?

Day 6: **Psalm 107** How does God respond to us in different situations? Do you see yourself in one of the ones described here?

____

____

✎ Take a few moments to journal your experience with prayer so far. Observe your progress with no judgment.

____

____

____

____

____

Prayer can have many forms. In the *Spiritual Disciplines Handbook*[12], there are fourteen different versions of prayer in the Prayer section. These include Breath Prayer, Centering Prayer, Inner-Healing Prayer, Praying Scripture, and Prayer Walking, along with others. Check out this resource for more information.

+ Spiritual Practice

The above Scriptures highlight the need to pray continually and sincerely. The following practices will help you deepen your prayer life and your relationship with God.

1. OFFERING SPACE FOR STILLNESS

BREATH PRAYER is a simple form of prayer that helps still our bodies and minds so we can become more centered and aware of God's presence. Praying with a sacred word or phrase along with your breath can quiet your mind, allowing you to connect more deeply with the Holy Spirit within. The Eastern Orthodox Church calls this the "Prayer of the Heart" or the "Jesus Prayer". The words are from Luke 18:38: "Lord Jesus Christ, have mercy on me, a sinner." This ancient practice coordinates the words with the rhythm of breathing.

I invite you this week to practice this simple prayer for five minutes to start. It might be helpful to use this prayer to still you before your daily Scripture readings or in the evening before bed to quiet your mind for rest. Choose a phrase, scripture, or prayer and coordinate it with your breath.

One way of doing this is to choose a name of God to breathe in and a desire or prayer of your heart to breathe out. Once you have this, settle into your space, realizing God is as close to you as your breath. Relax your body and become aware of your breathing. Slow your breathing down and begin your prayer—and continue for five minutes. You may find this simple prayer calling you at different times throughout your day.

Allow this practice to connect you with your inner sanctuary where God's Spirit dwells.

There is also an app for this called Centering Prayer.

2. OFFERING SPACE FOR CONVERSATION WITH GOD

Have you ever noticed that when people in the Bible encountered God or Jesus and heard what he said, they had questions and wanted to have a conversation? Prayer can be like this. Maybe you have questions about a Scripture passage and want to have a dialogue with God. Maybe you want to reflect on something from the previous exercise. Or perhaps you wish to have an honest conversation about something important in your life.

I invite you to try an ancient practice called the *Colloquy* or sacred conversation. Classically, this is used at the end of a time of Scripture meditation and prayer. At first, it may feel awkward, but with practice, it can really help you grow in your ability to hear and respond to God.

Choose a Scripture passage or a life situation and have a conversation with God, Jesus, or the Holy Spirit about it. As with any conversation, there is space to speak and listen. Journal your conversation, questions, and reflections during the Colloquy, and then listen for God's response.

____

____

____

____

____

____

3. CONTEMPLATE

He invites us into the living room of his heart,
where we can put on old slippers and share freely.
He invites us into the kitchen of his friendship,
where chatter and batter mix in good fun.
He invites us into the dining room of his strength,
where we can feast to our heart's delight.
He invites us into the study of his wisdom,
where we can learn and grow and stretch...
and ask all the questions we want.
He invites us into the workshop of his creativity,
where we can be co-laborers with him,
working together to determine the outcomes of events.
He invites us into the bedroom of his rest,
where new peace is found and where
we can be vulnerable and free.
(Richard Foster)

"The key to this home, this heart of God, is prayer...I am here to tell you that the Father's heart is open wide—you are welcome to come in."[13]

Consider Foster's description of the "rooms" in the Father's heart. Which room would you visit first? Why that one? Journal your thoughts.

____
____
____
____
____

♫ Music Meditation

When I Kneel to Pray is suggested as a possible way to continue your meditation as you go into the world. Listen to what speaks to you from the playlist on the *Come, Find Space with God* page. Listen to it several times this week.

? Questions for Reflection and Discussion

1. Reflect on your experience this week from your Spiritual Practices of Being Still, Listening, and Conversation with God. This could have been a challenge to implement. Be honest about both the frustrations and the blessings.

   ____
   ____
   ____
   ____
   ____

2. When you consider your definition of prayer from the beginning of this chapter, have there been any changes in perspective? Have you had any new insights on prayer? Do you sense the Spirit inviting you to explore different forms of prayer that will connect you in new ways with God during this season?

   ____
   ____
   ____

____

____

3. Was there a spiritual practice, scripture meditation, or reflection in this chapter that felt particularly important or resonated with you? Why? How did it affect your daily experience and finding space with God?

____

____

____

____

____

CHAPTER 4

Examen: Daily Discernment

What are some of the lessons you've learned in life? "Don't touch the hot stove or you'll get burned." Or "Don't run out in the road without looking for cars or you might get run over." "Share your toys." "Don't talk back."

How did you learn these lessons? Did you always believe the person who told you what you should or should not do—or did you have to experience the consequences first? Which of these—being told or learning by doing—is most effective?

Leoma's Story

When I taught English at the University of Khartoum, I quickly learned that my third- and fourth-year students had never once had graded work returned to them. No instructor had given out homework, graded it, and handed it back. The only evaluation came from the final examination—and those papers weren't given to them in case they decided to argue about how it was graded. As a result, many of my students couldn't write a complete sentence in English. They did not realize how little they knew.

I fixed that. I began giving homework assignments, had my students hand them in, and then marked them for each of my one hundred students. Then I gave a midterm examination. My students were very adept at cheating, so after a few years, I made up two versions of the exam and handed them out so that no one had the same test as their neighbor, though they looked very similar. I warned them that if they didn't take my midterm exam, they would probably fail the final exam and the course. Some of the cleverer students, as they handed in their midterm, would hesitantly ask me, "Were there two different tests?"

"Why?" I replied. "Were you looking at your neighbor's paper?" But of course, they were right.

One young man, a senior, failed my final exam. I was told to create a new exam so he could retake the test. He failed that one too. The following year, he took my exam again without having attended the class, as required by the regulations. He scored 17 out of 100. In desperation, he came to me and asked me to let him pass. Mine was the only course he had failed, and he needed the credit for his degree.

"Well," I asked, "what grade would you like? Do you want an A, or a B, perhaps a C? Why do we bother with all this teaching and testing? Just tell me what grade you want."

"Oh, I want to earn it!"

"Then study!"

He took his case all the way to the vice-chancellor's office. Upon request, I submitted my marking sheet along with his test, which made it clear he had not passed. He then asked the head of the English department to alter his grade. The head later told me that he advised the young man, "Wait until Dr. Leoma leaves and then try again." He knew I would not budge on the grade but thought whoever replaced me likely would.

What do you think happened to this young man? Was the result helpful? Why or why not? Like the students in Leoma's story who simply coast through life, not learning lessons, not growing and progressing, and trying to maneuver around taking responsibility, we too can sleepwalk through life. Granted, part of the problem in Leoma's story was a broken educational system that didn't allow the students to see their progress, or lack thereof, and make course corrections along the way. Also, the instructors allowed the students to be irresponsible, to cheat, and to move forward in mediocrity.

Many today aren't growing spiritually. The reasons could be similar to those described in Leoma's story.

1. Inadequate instruction
2. Inadequate review and reflection
3. Inadequate accountability

What if there was a way to learn, grow, reflect, make course corrections, and be accountable to God, ourselves, and perhaps a co-discerner/spiritual director or spiritual friend? What Leoma implemented with her students (periodic assignments, reflection, course correction, and accountability) can be helpful in our spiritual life. In this chapter, we introduce several Spiritual Practices to help us reflect, redirect, and restore us on our path.

Engaging with Scripture

[1] During the third year of King Jehoiakim's reign in Judah, King
Nebuchadnezzar of Babylon came to Jerusalem and besieged
it. [2] The Lord gave him victory over King Jehoiakim of Judah
and permitted him to take some of the sacred objects from the
Temple of God. So Nebuchadnezzar took them back to the land
of Babylonia and placed them in the treasure-house of his god. [3]
Then the king ordered Ashpenaz, his chief of staff, to bring to the
palace some of the young men of Judah's royal family and other
noble families, who had been brought to Babylon as captives. [4]
"Select only strong, healthy, and good-looking young men," he
said. "Make sure they are well versed in every branch of learning,
are gifted with knowledge and good judgment, and are suited to
serve in the royal palace. Train these young men in the language
and literature of Babylon." [5] The king assigned them a daily ra-
tion of food and wine from his own kitchens. They were to be
trained for three years, and then they would enter the royal service. [6] Daniel, Hananiah, Mishael, and Azariah were four of the
young men chosen, all from the tribe of Judah. [7] The chief of staff

renamed them with these Babylonian names: Daniel was called Belteshazzar. Hananiah was called Shadrach. Mishael was called Meshach. Azariah was called Abednego. [8] But Daniel was determined not to defile himself by eating the food and wine given to them by the king. He asked the chief of staff for permission not to eat these unacceptable foods. [9] Now God had given the chief of staff both respect and affection for Daniel. [10] But he responded, "I am afraid of my lord the king, who has ordered that you eat this food and wine. If you become pale and thin compared to the other youths your age, I am afraid the king will have me beheaded." [11] Daniel spoke with the attendant who had been appointed by the chief of staff to look after Daniel, Hananiah, Mishael, and Azariah. [12] "Please test us for ten days on a diet of vegetables and water," Daniel said. [13] "At the end of the ten days, see how we look compared to the other young men who are eating the king's food. Then make your decision in light of what you see." [14] The attendant agreed to Daniel's suggestion and tested them for ten days. [15] At the end of the ten days, Daniel and his three friends looked healthier and better nourished than the young men who had been eating the food assigned by the king. [16] So after that, the attendant fed them only vegetables instead of the food and wine provided for the others. [17] God gave these four young men an unusual aptitude for understanding every aspect of literature and wisdom. And God gave Daniel the special ability to interpret the meanings of visions and dreams. [18] When the training period ordered by the king was completed, the chief of staff brought all the young men to King Nebuchadnezzar. [19] The king talked with them, and no one impressed him as much as Daniel, Hananiah, Mishael, and Azariah. So they entered the royal service. [20] Whenever the king consulted them in any matter requiring wisdom and balanced judgment, he found them ten times more capable than any of the magicians and enchanters in his entire kingdom. (Daniel 1:1-20)

Reflection Questions

- What was Daniel's background?

  ____
  ____
  ____
  ____
  ____

- Suddenly, Daniel and his three friends found themselves in an awkward position. Taken by force to a foreign land, they were chosen to join the king's advisers and expected to eat the food at the royal table. So, what was the problem with that?

  ____
  ____
  ____
  ____
  ____

Daniel had been raised to eat kosher food. As Eagle[14] explains, "The three main rules of kosher are avoiding non-kosher animals, avoiding eating meat and dairy together, and ensuring meat is slaughtered according to Jewish law. Specifically, non-kosher animals include those without fins and scales (such as fish), those that don't chew the cud and have cloven hooves (including land animals), and most birds. Meat and dairy must be kept separate, both in preparation and consumption. Meat must also be slaughtered properly (shechita), and the blood must be drained."

- When Daniel and his friends realized what was expected of them, they had to decide what to do. How do you think that conversation went? What would you have done in their place?

____

____

____

____

____

This brings us to our practice for this chapter—examining your own life. Clinebill observes that the main reason to reappraise your lifestyle and values…is to ask yourself if you are on the road you really want to travel. [15] Will it take you where you want to end up?

Each day, life presents us with many lessons that we can learn. But if we don't take the time to think about what we experienced, we risk failing to learn—just as Leoma's student failed to understand what he needed to do to pass the course. Will you be successful and end up where you want to be? Or will you stumble through life, wondering why you don't succeed? The worst-case scenario would be to reach the end of your life and realize you never accomplished what you had hoped or planned.

The Examen

But there is hope. The Examen is a prayer practice that has been used for millennia. Pete Greig[16] describes its four steps as *Replay*, *Rejoice*, *Repent*, and *Reboot*. Let's consider each of these.

Replay

Some days, I can't remember what I did that morning, let alone yesterday or last week. To get the most out of my Examen, I take time before I go to bed to think back on my day. I like to ask the question, "Where did I see God today?" You might also ask, "Where did I see kindness, or honesty, or blessing?" Spend a few minutes reflecting on these moments.

Rejoice

Consider the good things that happened to you during the day—food to eat, clothes to wear, work to do. Where did you find joy? Perhaps you helped someone with a problem, saw a beautiful scene in nature, or received a compliment from a colleague or friend. Where did you give or receive nourishment for your soul? Reflect on those moments and how they made you feel.

Repent

Now go back over your day once more. Were there times when you could have handled a situation better? Perhaps you became angry or resentful. Maybe someone hurt you or challenged you. Would Jesus be pleased with how you lived out your day? Was there a kindness you could have done but didn't? As you confess these moments to yourself and to God, ask for forgiveness and determine to do better tomorrow. As Richard Foster[17] reminds us, it can be hard to confess a wrong because once we admit to a sin, the next challenge is to stop doing it.

Reboot

Having seen where you did well and where you need to improve and having been forgiven for what you did or failed to do, you can begin again. Tomorrow is a new day. God's mercies are new every morning, and his faithfulness is great. Rest in God's unfailing love.

Scripture Meditation

The readings for this week suggest ways we can examine ourselves and walk closely with God. The Examen practice offers a concrete way to do this daily.

Journal your thoughts and reflections from these passages.

Day 1: **Proverbs 1** Solomon is known for his wisdom. What advice and warnings do you find here?

Day 2: **Proverbs 2** What are the benefits of wisdom according to Solomon?

Day 3: **Psalm 46** What resources are promised when life gets complicated?

Day 4: **Isaiah 6:1-8** What made Isaiah aware of his sin?

Day 5: **Romans 7:14-8:4** Do you feel the struggle that Paul describes? What solution does Paul find?

Day 6: **James 1:19-27** What warnings does James give us?

+ Spiritual Practice

1. THE EXAMEN PRAYER

The practice that has been used for millennia is called the Examen. Start the Examen by prayerfully becoming aware of God's presence with you, quieting yourself, and asking the Holy Spirit to guide your prayer time as you reflect on your day and become aware of God's loving gaze upon you.

Here are several simple steps to guide you in praying your daily Examen. You can use this format or Greig's 4 R's (replay, rejoice, repent, reboot). Use whichever resonates with you.

1. Start with Gratitude for several things, both big and small, you notice from your day.
2. Next, slowly review your day with the Holy Spirit, from morning to evening. Notice where you sensed God's presence and where you felt disconnected. What interior movements did you observe—feelings, longings, repulsions, and distractions? Ask the Holy Spirit to highlight and deepen your understanding of a moment or feeling from the day.
3. Savor the moments and feelings of God's presence with gratitude.
4. Ask forgiveness for moments in your day where you resisted God's presence and action.

5. Ask God to offer you grace for tomorrow and guidance toward practical ways to move forward with what has been revealed to you.

Here is a short six-minute video about the Examen Prayer:

Examen prayer

This is a short guided Examen you can try. If you need more time, simply pause the video.

Guided Examen

✎ You may find it helpful to journal anything that was especially meaningful from your Examen exercises. This can assist you in seeing patterns and progress, as well as answered prayer.

There is also an Examen app you can download.

2. CONFESSION TO A SAFE PERSON

Sometimes we discover something in our lives that weighs us down with guilt and shame or hinders us in other ways. Bringing these discoveries into the light with a trusted spiritual mentor, director, priest or friend, and then receiving a blessing of forgiveness can truly set us free and help move us forward on our life's journey and our relationship with God.

Is there something specific that the Holy Spirit is highlighting in your life as a possible obstacle to your relationship with God and your spiritual growth? Consider bringing it into the light of confession.

When considering a trusted person to bring your confession to, it's usually best if they are spiritually mature, confidential, and nonjudgmental. Don't choose someone within your immediate family or someone prone to gossip.

♫ Music Meditation

Peace Over You by Dustin Smith and James Galbraith is suggested as a possible way to continue your meditation as you go into the world. Listen to what speaks to you, listening to it several times this week.

? Questions for Reflection and Discussion

1. While practicing the examen prayer, was there anything surprising or perhaps disturbing that the Holy Spirit highlighted on a particular day? Where did you notice God's grace and presence with you? Was there a theme or pattern you observed about your days?

   ____

   ____

   ____

   ____

   ____

2. Was there a spiritual practice, scripture meditation, or reflection in this chapter that felt particularly important or resonated with you? Why? How did it affect your daily experience and finding space with God?

____

____

____

____

____

CHAPTER 5

Discernment: Decision-making

What decisions have you had to make recently? Some choices are small, while others can make a lifelong difference. Deciding what to have for lunch is less significant than choosing a job. *Should I change jobs or stay where I am? Should I date, marry, or divorce this person? How should I raise my children—or should I have children at all? Which treatment should I choose for this illness?*

Decisions shape our lives. But the real question is: how do you know whether you should—or shouldn't—do something?

Leoma's Story

When I began hosting people long-term in my small two-bedroom house, I questioned my decision multiple times. There always seem to be teenagers involved—an unfamiliar experience for me.

God assured me that He had already prepared me to share my life with others, as I had never lived alone during my years in Africa. And in Sudan, living alone would send all kinds of wrong signals. Still, inviting others into my home would be financially costly as well as emotionally draining for me as an introvert. My schedule was interrupted repeatedly, and for months, I had to focus on solving their problems, totally setting aside my personal goals. I just couldn't handle both. It was painful not to make any progress on my goals along with watching their suffering as we hit wall after wall.

After a frustrating morning where all answers were "no," even my garage door refused to open.

"Even the garage door is saying 'No'!" I cried out.

Yet, slowly, the pieces began to come together. There are still major challenges but also hope.

God asks us to open ourselves to Him—but He doesn't stop there. He may also ask us to open our wallets, our time, our homes, and our hearts to others. Will those actions cost us? Yes. Will sacrifice be involved? Absolutely. Will there be pain? Likely. But what is the reward?

God says He created each of us for a purpose. What is yours? It may take some time to discover it and implement it, but as we offer space for God in our lives, He reveals the gifts and passions He created in us—and more skills will develop along the way. Once we identify our calling and follow it, our lives will never be the same.

From personal experience, I can testify that while my life has held many challenges, I have found peace, contentment, and fulfillment. Would I do it again? In a heartbeat!

God is no one's debtor. What we experience here, however difficult, can't compare with what God is preparing for us.

Engaging with Scripture

6 "For God, who said, 'Let there be light
in the darkness,' has made this light
shine in our hearts so we could know
the glory of God that is seen in the face
of Jesus Christ. 7 We now have this light
shining in our hearts, but we ourselves
are like fragile clay jars containing this
great treasure. This makes it clear that our great power is from
God, not from ourselves. 8 We are pressed on every side by troubles, but we are not crushed. We are perplexed but not driven to

despair. [9] We are hunted down but never abandoned by God. We get knocked down, but we are not destroyed. [10] Through suffering, our bodies continue to share in the death of Jesus so that the life of Jesus may also be seen in our bodies."

(2 Corinthians 4:6-10)

Do you ever feel like a fragile clay jar? What events in life make you feel that way—work, family, expectations from others?

Verse 7 tells of a great treasure. What is that treasure, and how did it help Paul? When we find ourselves in a hard place, do we think of it as a punishment, as discouragement, or as a time to turn to God? When do we learn the most about Him—in easy times or amid hard situations? Why?

[16] That is why we never give up. Though our bodies are dying, our spirits are being renewed every day. [17] For our present troubles are small and won't last very long. Yet they produce for us a glory that vastly outweighs them and will last forever! [18] So we don't look at the troubles we can see now; rather, we fix our gaze on things that cannot be seen. For the things we see now will soon be gone, but the things we cannot see will last forever. (2 Corinthians 4:16-18)

Reflection Questions

- What advice do we see in these verses? How can this perspective change our view of today's problems?

  ____

  ____

  ____

  ____

  ____

- What if God puts a challenging opportunity in your path? Do you have to accept it? Reject it? How do you decide?

Here are some things to consider:

- Are there ways God has prepared you to take on this challenge?
- Are the needed resources available?
- Do you have experience in this area?
- Has God given you spiritual gifts that will make a difference in this situation?

Scripture Meditation

You may use these scriptures to consider how you and God relate regarding discernment.

Day 1: **Nehemiah 2:1-8** What did Nehemiah risk by asking the world's most powerful person for help?

Day 2: **Psalm 139** What does God know about you? What has God planned for you?

Day 3: **Ephesians 4: 11-16** How do we become mature?

Day 4: **Romans 12:2-8** How has God provided for his people to carry out his work?

Day 5: **James 1:2-8** Is there value in trouble? How should we handle challenges?

Day 6: **James 1:19-27** What does God say about works, faith, and priorities?

Has God taught you anything through these verses? What do you think He is inviting you to do?

✎Take time to note your thoughts.

Sometimes the direction God gives is hard, yet we are given this promise:

[17] For our present troubles are small and won't last very long. Yet **they produce for us a glory that vastly outweighs them and will last forever!** [18] So we don't look at the troubles we can see now; rather, we **fix our gaze on things that cannot be seen.** For the things we see now will soon be gone, but **the things we cannot see will last forever.** (2 Corinthians 4:17-18)

+ Spiritual Practice

The verses suggested for the daily readings emphasize wisdom, guidance, and the importance of God's direction. The practices that follow will help you discern his voice more clearly in your daily life.

Offering Space for Discernment

Did you know *discernment* is an ancient spiritual practice within Christianity? It was—and is—used not only for making decisions, but also to determine vocation and callings.

Back in the 1500s, St. Ignatius of Loyola developed Three Modes of Discernment[18].

The First Mode of Discernment is the simplest. A decision feels certain, and you don't have doubts. You have clarity and peace about the decision

The Second Mode of Discernment is more complex and requires a process. First, you pray about the decision with a spiritual director or friend. While praying and thinking about the decision, notice the inner movements of your soul. Are you experiencing *consolation*—feelings of inner freedom, peace, and hope?

Also notice if you are experiencing *desolation*—anything that moves you toward hopelessness. Are you agitated or restless? As Ignatius puts it, are you "listless, tepid, and unhappy?" These sensations likely mean you are moving toward a bad decision.

Another way to discern in the second mode is to use your imagination to place yourself in each possible decision for a few days. Notice which one moves you toward greater inner peace, freedom, and joy.

This discernment process can be tricky because our hearts can deceive us if we are moving away from God. We might also be too attached to a particular outcome. Because of this, it's wise to start our discernment process by praying for *holy indifference* or *detachment*. This includes daily reading and study of Scripture.

The Third Mode of Discernment can be the most difficult. Perhaps you have two or three good or moderate options. Things seem muddled and unclear, and you don't sense either spiritual consolation or desolation.

We won't get into the process here, but James Martin goes into more detail in *The Jesuit Guide to (Almost) Anything*[19].

PRACTICE 1

Consider setting aside several prayer times this week to reflect on a decision or possible vocational calling. Start by asking the Holy Spirit to guide you in your prayer through Consolation or Desolation. Pay attention to your inner movements and feelings. Do they bring you faith, peace, and hope, or agitation, restlessness, and hopelessness? Journal your experience.

You may want to use the Feeling Wheel app to further pinpoint your inner feelings.

Along with this discernment practice, pay special attention to how Scripture guides you. A large part of discernment for Christians is becoming more familiar with God's word. "But solid food is for the mature, for those who have their powers of discernment trained by constant practice to distinguish good from evil." (Hebrews 5:14, ESV)

PRACTICE 2

What if God puts a challenging opportunity in your path? Do you have to accept it? reject it? How do you decide?

Here are some possible things to consider:

- Are there ways God has prepared you to take on this challenge?
- Are the resources needed available?
- Do you have experience in this area?
- Has God given you spiritual gifts that will make a difference in this situation?

Here are a few scriptures listing spiritual gifts: Romans 12, 1 Corinthians 12-14, and Ephesians 4. Ask those close to you what your spiritual gifts are.

✎ Journal your thoughts.

____

____

____

____

____

? Questions for Reflection and Discussion

A big question people have asked throughout the ages is: "What is my purpose? What am I here for?" Does God have a purpose for me? Is it pre-ordained and set or do I have a role to play in discovering it? These are big questions you might have asked.

Albert Haase[20] has a chapter on Discernment that I, Carol, found helpful, especially the part about our hopes, dreams, and desires, as well as God's Dream. Haase emphasized God's dream as a dream of peace, justice, and love with us as stewards. We cooperate with God in this dream, and it can connect with our dreams and longings.

To take some pressure off, he says:

> God's will is not some predetermined, preordained decision from on high that we must struggle to figure out and then buckle under to obey...Rather, we are left to freely shape the gift of life of the original dream for all creation...The very fact that the garden of Eden was a paradise hints at God's dream. All creation was interrelated and interdependent like an intricate spider's web. God's presence was so immediate that God could be heard walking in the garden at the time of the evening breeze, Genesis 3:8. Indeed, creation was "very good," (1:31) ... Through our upbringing, talents, abilities, and deepest desires, God presents us with a canvas, paint, and brushes. We become the artists of our own lives. Discerning God's will is nothing more than responding to a situation with our unique, gifted contribution to God's dream for creation.[21]

1. Why are you here on this earth? Does God have a purpose for you? (Often, we will discover God's purpose through listening to our deep inner longings and dreams. These may get buried in the busyness of life and others' expectations. Consider taking extra time to reconnect inwardly

with these sacred longings and journal what you hear and see. Maybe even schedule a day away for retreat, or if time doesn't allow this, perhaps a morning or afternoon mini retreat.) If you listened for dreams and longings, what did you hear or notice? How did your dreams interact with God's dream?

2. Have you experienced a challenging time in life that you felt God may have invited you to offer hospitality or actively help someone in need? How did you grow during this time? How did God seem present or absent during your experience? What lessons did you learn? Journal your reflections.

3. Was there a spiritual practice, scripture meditation, or reflection in this chapter that felt particularly important or resonated with you? Why? How did it affect your daily experience and finding space with God?

CHAPTER 6

Surrender: Accepting God's Plan

Have you ever told God, I'll do anything except ..." Or, maybe you've said, "I'll never do ..." What often happens? Sometimes those are just the things God wants you to do. But what if you don't want to do what God asks of you?

Leoma's Story

My mother dedicated me to the Lord when I was a child. We went to a Baptist church, so they didn't offer infant baptism. However, as I grew, I felt God calling me to be a missionary. My response? "Just don't send me to Africa!" And guess where I ended up?

When the time came to make the decision, I must admit that I did not want to go to Africa—particularly Kenya. God and I had a long argument while I sat high in the branches of a tree. In the end, God won. I headed to Kenya but ended up in Sudan. Ironically, although I had avoided learning Arabic, my first nine months there were spent studying that language. Afterward, I moved to a Shilluk village. I lived there for a few weeks, but then a civil war started and I had to evacuate. I told God I didn't want to leave. He assured me he understood—but I would never see that place again. I wept at that answer.

Later, I moved to Khartoum and worked for many years with the Shilluks and other language groups. In 1996, I began teaching at the University of Khartoum in addition to my other work. It was hard, but I had never felt so fulfilled.

Then in 2002, my mother became frail and needed me at home. I didn't want to leave my meaningful work in Khartoum, but God told me I was needed elsewhere—not the message I wanted to hear. We argued about that for two years, but once again, God won. I was home with my mother for eight years before she transitioned to heaven.

In the meantime, God provided me with another even more impactful role in Africa. These changes of direction, while painful, gave God space to redirect my life.

Engaging with Scripture

32 They went to the olive grove called Gethsemane, and Jesus said,
"Sit here while I go and pray." 33 He took Peter, James, and John
with him, and he became deeply troubled and distressed. 34 He
told them, "My soul is crushed with grief to the point of death.
Stay here and keep watch with me." 35 He went on a little farther
and fell to the ground. He prayed that, if it were possible, the
awful hour awaiting him might pass him by. 36 "Abba, Father,"
he cried out, "everything is possible for you. Please take this cup
of suffering away from me. Yet I want your will to be done, not
mine." (Mark 14:32-36)

Reflection Questions

Pete Greig[22] points out that Jesus repeatedly asked God to find another way for him to redeem the world. Jesus cried out, "Everything is possible for you." But in the end, he said, "Not my will, but yours be done."

This is a striking example of Jesus desperately seeking to avoid doing what God had sent him to do. Jesus didn't want to do it. He said, "My soul is crushed with grief to the point of death." Matthew 26:38. At any point, Jesus could have called for rescue and been released from the suffering and shame of the cross. But he didn't. Instead, as Hebrews 12:2 (NIV) says, "For the joy set before Him, he endured the cross, despising the shame, and sat down at the right hand of the throne of God."

What was that joy? It was knowing that by his completion of this most difficult act, he freed many from sin and death and enabled them to live with him for eternity.

So, when God tells you to do something that you really don't want to do, how should you respond?

- **First**, make sure you have correctly heard what God has told you to do.
- **Next,** be honest with your loving Father, telling him, "I don't want to do this."
- **Then,** listen for God to affirm his request and help you see why this is the best path for you right now. Remember God's promise in Jeremiah 29:11 that he knows the plans he has for you—plans for good and not for evil, to give you a future and a hope.
- **Finally,** pray "Your will be done on earth as it is in heaven."

Carol's Story A Process of Surrender

When I was in my thirties, I sensed God leading me to homeschool my children. I noticed excitement and confusion. The positives came through people, circumstances, scripture, and even media highlighting homeschooling. These seemed like confirmations of what I was hearing from God. But I still felt conflicted, both internally and externally. I needed to decide how to navigate the obstacles while remembering the confirmations.

My first hurdle involved arguing with God. It went something like this: *Are you kidding, God? All the other moms will send their kids off to school and have freedom for a few hours in the day. Also, I know nothing about teaching and never trained as a teacher or imagined myself teaching.*

Little by little, God assured me of His presence and guidance.

The next obstacle was my husband. He did not like the idea of homeschooling. *Really God, are you sure you want this to happen?*

One night, I prayed that if God wanted this to happen, he would have to change my husband's heart and mind about homeschooling. Guess what? The next day, he came home from work and said that a man had told him about his own homeschooling experience. My husband said he had decided he liked the idea. *What*?!

My experiences haven't always been that dramatic, but in this instance, I had a choice to surrender and submit to God or go my own stubborn way. Looking back, I am so glad I allowed God to open up space for wonderful adventures with God and my children that I wouldn't otherwise have had.

Scripture Meditation

Consider each person in the following verses. What was asked of them that they didn't want to do? What did they do in the end? How did it turn out for them?

✎ Don't forget to write your reflections.

Day 1: **Exodus 3:7-15**

____

____

____

____

____

Day 2: **1 Samuel 15:1-23**

____

____

____

____

____

Day 3: **Genesis 22:1-18**

Day 4: **Esther 4:7-17**

Day 5: **John 18:15-18, 25-27, 21:15-19**

Day 6: **2 Corinthians 12:1-10**

+ Spiritual Practice

The Scriptures remind us of the challenge—and the gift—of yielding to God's will. The next practice will help you explore surrender as a step toward deeper trust in Him.

So, when we believe God is telling us to do something that we really don't want to do, what should our process be?

We want to make sure we have correctly heard what God has told us to do.

In the last chapter, we focused on discernment by noticing Consolation and Desolation. In this example of Jesus's life and in hard situations for us, it may be much more difficult to discern through this process alone. We may only feel desolation and struggle. However, when God calls us, by the end of the process, we want to discern God's presence, grace, and peace. We need to draw close to God in prayer. Often, we won't discern God's purpose for tough decisions until we look back and notice the good that comes from obeying God in the challenge.

How do we know we have heard God accurately and not our inner critic guilting us into action or our fears preventing inner freedom?

It isn't always easy to know for sure, but as you grow in your relationship with God and practice listening for the Spirit's still small voice, you will gain confidence. You may notice God speaking in various ways such as scripture, sacred reading, dreams and visions, songs, prayer, circumstances, and others. The Holy Spirit may bring you conviction, challenge, comfort, encouragement, invitation, and courage. On the other hand, the Enemy of our souls can bring condemnation, accusation, fear, discouragement, and seem pushy, harsh, or forceful. When making big decisions, it is best not to rush. Seek wise counsel or spiritual direction.

- Practice this week, noticing invitations in your life from God through the Spirit's still small voice and similar messages through sources such as those listed above. Also, be aware of the inner and outer obstacles the Enemy may bring to you, such as those listed above. Journal your reflections.
- We can honestly talk to our loving Father, telling him, "I don't want to do this." Listen for God to affirm his request to you and help you see why this is the best option for

you right now. God promises us in Jeremiah 29:11 that he knows the plans he has for you, plans for good and not for evil, to give you a future and a hope.

- Consider having an authentic colloquy with God, Jesus, or the Holy Spirit as described in Chapter 3 on prayer. You can voice your sadness, fears, and anger knowing God still loves you. The Psalms are excellent examples of prayers to God expressing all kinds of feelings.
- Finally, pray "Your will be done on earth as it is in heaven."

This type of surrender is one of the most difficult, yet results in the healing, freeing, and maturing aspects of our spiritual journey. St. Ignatius of Loyola would call this concept "The Principle and Foundation" or the Prayer of Indifference or Detachment. Here is a definition of Ignatian Indifference, "The grace-filled state of desiring to do God's will and to praise, reverence, and serve God more than desiring anything else. The state of grateful availability."[23]

While taking spiritual directees through the nine-month Ignatian Retreat in Everyday Life I sometimes suggest that they pray for God's gift of grace for indifference. This could be a prayer for you as you discern direction for your life. This grace-filled gift of detachment can bring freedom to do God's will with more peace, clarity, love, and presence. Indifference to our preferences and attachments isn't something we can produce ourselves, which is why we need God's grace.

Here are two examples of the "Principle and Foundation" to reflect upon. Once reading these, consider writing your own "Principle and Foundation" and praying for God's grace to help you.

Traditional Translation

God created human beings to praise, reverence, and serve God, and by doing this, to save their souls. God created all other things on the face of the earth to help fulfill this purpose.

It follows that we are to use the things of this world only if they help us to this end, and we ought to rid ourselves of the things of this world when they impede this end.

For this it is necessary to make ourselves indifferent to all created things as much as we are able, so that we do not necessarily want health rather than sickness, riches rather than poverty, honor rather than dishonor, a long rather than a short life, and so in all the rest, so that we ultimately desire and choose only what is most conducive for us to the end for which God created us.

Contemporary Translation

God created us to share life with us forever. Our love response takes shape in our praise, honor, and service to God in our life.

All the things of this world are also created because of God's love, and they become a context of gifts, presented to us so that we can know God more easily and make a return of love more readily.

As a result, we show reverence for all the gifts of creation and collaborate with God in using them so that by being good stewards we develop as loving persons in our care for God's world and its development. But if we abuse any of these gifts of creation or, on the contrary, take them as the center of our lives, we break our relationship with God and hinder our growth as persons.

In everyday life, then, we must hold ourselves in balance before all created gifts insofar as we have a choice and are not bound by some responsibility. We should not fix our desires on health or sickness, wealth or poverty, success or failure, a long life or a short one. For everything has the potential of calling forth in us a more loving response to our life forever with God.

Our only desire and our one choice should be this: I want and I choose what better leads to God's deepening life in me.[24]

♫ Music Meditation

Several songs are suggested as a possible way to continue your meditation as you go into the world: *Your Way's Better* by Forrest Frank, *Jesus I Believe* by Big Daddy Weave, *Everlasting Love* by Bridgette Smisor Shevy. Listen to what speaks to you, listening to it several times this week.

? Questions for Reflection and Discussion

1. As you reflect on Leoma's and Carol's stories and consider your own journey so far; can you relate at all to ever sensing God calling you to do anything you didn't want to or didn't feel equipped to do? What was that like if so?

   ____
   ____
   ____
   ____
   ____

2. Was there a spiritual practice, scripture meditation or reflection that particularly felt important or that resonated with you from your time in this chapter? Why? How did it affect your daily experience and finding space with God?

   ____
   ____
   ____
   ____
   ____

3. Finally, reflect on Thomas Merton's prayer[25] and whether you resonate with it.

____

My Lord God,
I have no idea where I am going.
I do not see the road ahead of me.
I cannot know for certain where it will end.
Nor do I really know myself,
and the fact that I think that I am following your will
does not mean that I am actually doing so.
But I believe that the desire to please you
does in fact please you.
And I hope I have that desire in all that I am doing.
I hope that I will never do anything apart from that desire.
And I know that if I do this you will lead me by the right road,
though I may know nothing about it.
Therefore, I will trust you always,
though I may seem to be lost and in the shadow of death.
I will not fear,
for you are ever with me,
and you will never leave me to face my perils alone.
—Thomas Merton

CHAPTER 7

Evaluating our Thoughts and Plans

You've probably heard the saying "Sticks and stones may break my bones, but words will never hurt me." That's one of the biggest lies ever taught to children. Words can hurt deeply. Even more damaging than the words others say to us are the words we say to ourselves.

What words do you hear most often in your mind? Did they come from a parent, sibling, teacher, or "friend"? Why do you repeat them? Do you really believe them? Are they true?

In this chapter, we will consider how our inner voices affect us, and how a spiritual director can assist us to think God's thoughts.

Leoma's Story

In my early years, when I made a mistake—dropped a dish, failed to perform perfectly—I would say to myself: *You are stupid. What a clumsy oaf! That was dumb. I'm a failure.* Yes, I had done something wrong, but we all make mistakes—that's what learning is all about. None of us gets through life without erring. Putting myself down was a way of punishing myself, and the self-criticism made me feel worthless, hopelessly inept, and undeserving.

While I was memorizing Romans, Chapter 8 hit me hard. What was I thinking? Did my self-talk reflect what God thought of me? It was as if God said, "*Stop that kind of thinking*!" God made me, and my goal as a Christian is to honor what He is doing in my life. There is no place for negative self-talk, especially when it isn't true.

Years later, while working in my kitchen in Juba, Sudan—I think I was butchering a piece of buffalo leg—God challenged me again. I had a sharp tongue and joked with people in ways that were hurtful. My comments were barbed, and I knew it. I felt God saying, "*Stop that! You're hurting people.*" From that day on, I have become more careful about what I say and how I say it. I'm not perfect, but at least I'm moving in a more thoughtful direction.

As an author, I sometimes suffer from impostor syndrome—persistent feelings of inadequacy, self-doubt, and fear of being exposed as a fraud despite evidence to the contrary. When I considered speaking on podcasts, producing short videos, or speaking at public gatherings, fears arose in my mind. *What do I have to say that anyone would want to hear? Do I really know enough about this?*

At times like these, I've found spiritual direction very helpful. A spiritual director listens to the directee, and then, as the Spirit leads, asks questions. Are the concerns being expressed in line with God's Word? What is the motivation? How would these actions or thoughts glorify God?

When my thoughts take me down a rabbit hole or have me chasing squirrels, a spiritual director helps me refocus on the actual issue and solutions. In short, we are not always our best counselors—sometimes we need outside perspective to keep us on the right track.

A spiritual director can:

- help you grow in awareness and a deeper connection to the Holy Spirit's movement in your life.
- provide a safe space to process questions and struggles on your faith journey.

- offer spiritual discernment during transitions or times of feeling stuck in life.
- provide sacred companionship during deconstructing and / or reconstructing faith.
- assist in discerning your longings, identity, and callings.
- suggest spiritual practices and rhythms that fit who you are and where you are on your journey.

Perhaps you can relate to one or two of these and might benefit from spiritual direction. The sacred listening of spiritual companionship can help you untangle your thoughts, feelings, desires, and circumstances, making you more aware of God's presence and the Spirit's still, small voice. Ultimately, it can help you with life's struggles and challenges—however, the healing and growth come from the focus of each session being presence-centered rather than problem-centered.

Engaging with Scripture

1 In the days when the judges ruled in Israel, a severe famine came upon the land. So, a man from Bethlehem in Judah left his home and went to live in the country of Moab, taking his wife and two sons with him. 2 The man's name was Elimelech, and his wife was Naomi. Their two sons were Mahlon and Kilion. They were Ephrathites from Bethlehem in the land of Judah. And when they reached Moab, they settled there. 3 Then Elimelech died, and Naomi was left with her two sons. 4 The two sons married Moabite women. One married a woman named Orpah, and the other a woman named Ruth. But about ten years later, 5 both Mahlon and Kilion died. This left Naomi alone, without her two sons or her husband. 6 Then Naomi heard in Moab that the LORD had blessed his people in Judah by giving them good crops again. So, Naomi and her daughters-in-law got ready to leave Moab to return to her homeland. 7 With her two daughters-in-law she

set out from the place where she had been living, and they took the road that would lead them back to Judah. [8] But on the way, Naomi said to her two daughters-in-law, "Go back to your mothers' homes. And may the LORD reward you for your kindness to your husbands and to me. [9] May the LORD bless you with the security of another marriage." Then she kissed them good-bye, and they all broke down and wept...[16] But Ruth replied, "Don't ask me to leave you and turn back. Wherever you go, I will go; wherever you live, I will live. Your people will be my people, and your God will be my God. [17] Wherever you die, I will die, and there I will be buried. May the LORD punish me severely if I allow anything but death to separate us!" [18] When Naomi saw that Ruth was determined to go with her, she said nothing more. [19] So the two of them continued on their journey. When they came to Bethlehem, the entire town was excited by their arrival. "Is it really Naomi?" the women asked. [20] "Don't call me Naomi," she responded. "Instead, call me Mara, for the Almighty has made life very bitter for me. [21] I went away full, but the LORD has brought me home empty. Why call me Naomi when the LORD has caused me to suffer and the Almighty has sent such tragedy upon me?" (Ruth 1:1-9, 16-21)

Reflection Questions

- What words do you think Naomi had in her head while she lived in Moab?

- Why would Naomi insist her daughters-in-law return to their mothers' homes?

- What messages might have been going through Naomi's mind about herself and her situation?

- What is the significance of wanting to change her name to Mara (bitter)?

- What did Ruth see in her mother-in-law that made her stay with Naomi?

Scripture Meditation

You may use these verses to find ways to bring your thought-life under God's control.

Day 1: **James 3:2-12** Why must we guard our tongues (as well as our thoughts)?

Day 2: **Philippians 4:6-9** Are your thoughts fixed on the things listed here?

Day 3: **Romans 8:12-17** As God's adopted children, how should we think of ourselves?

Day 4: **Proverbs 18** List the positive and negative terms used regarding words.

Day 5: **Proverbs 4** What is the value of wise advice?

Day 6: **Matthew 7: 24-27** Are you listening to wise teaching and following it?

+ Spiritual Direction

Consider how a spiritual director might be a companion with you in your life and inner journey.

Here are some quotes on Spiritual Direction that may help you understand this ministry better. You can also find more information at: www.soulssanctuaryspiritualdirection.com

- "Spiritual direction is a prayer process in which a person seeking help in cultivating a deeper personal relationship with God meets with another for prayer and conversation that is focused on increasing awareness of God in the midst of life experiences."[26]
- "Spiritual Direction is designed to help directees listen to God—who desires relationship and who longs for people to express the truth of who they are as they share their gifts, experience, and personhood with others."[27]
- "Christian spiritual direction is a process whereby one individual—the director—is welcomed into the life-story of another—the directee—past, present, and future. The

directee enters a relationship of trust with his or her director, and the latter agrees to walk with that person on his or her 'faith journey through life."[28]

- "The main questions for spiritual direction—Who am I? Where have I come from? And where am I going? What is prayer? Who is God for me? How does God speak to me? Where do I belong? How can I be of service? —are not questions with simple answers but questions that lead us deeper into the unspeakable mystery of existence."[29]
- "The primary focus of spiritual direction is on religious experience, not ideas, and how this experience touches the most profound level of the person. It is concerned with the inner life, that dimension of existence that deals with the heart, and the deep feeling states that arise from the closeness of the person to his or her divine source."[30]

+ Spiritual Quote Reflection

Read the reflection below slowly several times in the style of *lectio divina*. As you do, meditate on what the Holy Spirit highlights for you.

> "It is impossible for the mind not to be troubled by thoughts, but accepting or rejecting them is possible for everyone who makes an effort. It is true that their origin does not in every respect depend on us, but it is equally true that their refusal or acceptance does depend on us...
>
> "This activity of the heart is not inappropriately compared to millstones, which the swift rush of waters turns with a violent revolving motion. As long as the water's force keeps them spinning they are utterly incapable of stopping their work, but it is in the power of the one who supervises to decide whether to grind wheat, or barley, or darnel.

Indeed, only that will be ground which has been accepted by the person entrusted with responsibility for the work." [31]

+ Spiritual Practices

These verses remind us how powerful our thoughts and words can be—both in shaping our own lives and those of others. The following spiritual practices will help you notice and redirect your thoughts, so they align with God's truth.

1. Finding space with God to show you your limiting beliefs and negative self-talk

Some examples of false or limiting beliefs and negative self-talk are: I am *not worthy, I am stupid, I am not good enough, I am ugly, I am too old, I am too young,* etc.

This week, ask God to show you your most prominent limiting beliefs and negative self-talk. Consider setting aside time for quiet reflection to listen for what the Holy Spirit reveals to you. Write down what you discover. Which one or two beliefs are most prominent for you? Sit with this thought. Do they have an emotion attached to them? Where do you feel them in your body? Ask the thought or belief what it wants to tell you and write it down. Then ask God how He sees you. Reflect on His answer. Ask God to show you a more empowering belief, thought, or Scripture. Write this down on a card to keep with you and meditate on.

2. Offering space to breathe with the Holy Spirit

Once you are aware of your false or limiting beliefs and thoughts, practice using a *Breath Prayer Affirmation* to breathe out the negative talk and breathe in the true, life-giving thoughts, words, or phrases God shows you. Use this prayer practice throughout the week—especially when you catch yourself in negative self-talk. Eventually, you may find yourself praying only the affirmation prayer, removing the negative one.

Here are some examples (or create your own):

- Breathe Out- *I am not good enough* — Breathe In- *I am perfectly and wonderfully made*
  (Then - In- *I am perfectly* — Out - *and wonderfully made*)
- Breathe Out - *I am stupid* — Breathe In - *I have the mind of Christ*
  (Then - In- *I have* — Out - *the mind of Christ*)

3. Daily Examen

One of my directees created her own Daily Examen based on Philippians 4:4-9. Consider trying this once, twice, or each evening this week:

- *Rejoice in the Lord always. Again, I say, rejoice!*
  What am I grateful for today? Be specific. Give thanks.
- *Let your gentleness be evident to all...*
  How can I bring joy and encouragement into life today? Be specific. Allow the Holy Spirit to mention people. What would bring me joy and encouragement today?
- *Do not be anxious about anything.*
  What sharp movements will the evil one bring to you today? Recognize them and turn into prayer.
- *...but by prayer and petition, with thanksgiving, in every situation, present your requests to God.*
  Ask God to help you with tasks/problems you expect to encounter today. List them.

- *And the peace that passes all understanding will guard your mind in Jesus Christ.*
  Were you troubled today? If so, have you followed these steps? Have you kept your eyes on Jesus? Walked in gratitude? Focused on what is lovely, just, worthy of praise, commendable, noble, and pure?

Whatever you have learned from Jesus, put it into practice. The God of peace will be with you.

Colloquy: What actions or decisions today have drawn you toward Christ? Which pulled you away?

____

____

____

____

____

♫ Music Meditation

Alongside Scripture, prayer, and spiritual practices, music can be a powerful tool for meditation. Let "*Near to Hear*" by Songs of Wisdom guide you into reflection and prayer. Go to the playlist and listen to it several times this week.

? Questions for Reflection and Discussion

1. When you ponder your false beliefs and negative self-talk, ask God to show you if there are strong emotions attached to these beliefs or past wounds and traumas associated with them. Ask Him to heal you and set you free. Journal your reflections. Consider seeking healing prayer, spiritual direction, or counseling, if needed.

   ____

   ____

   ____

____

____

2. Here are some spiritual direction questions to ask yourself. Where did I notice God's action and presence in my life this week? When did I move toward God's action? When did I resist? Journal your thoughts.

____

____

____

____

____

3. Was there a spiritual practice, scripture meditation, or reflection in this chapter that felt particularly important or resonated with you? Why? How did it affect your daily experience and finding space with God?

____

____

____

____

____

CHAPTER 8

Scripture Memory: Revitalizing Your Soul

Moving from being a dependent to an independent adult is full of pitfalls. As a twenty-something-year-old man told me, "You don't know what you can do until you get out there and find out." Adulting isn't the magical freedom it may appear to be. In fact, many of us make our worst mistakes during this period. What mistakes have you made that you now regret? What are ways you have found to avoid heading down the wrong path?

Leoma's Story

I learned adulting the hard way, as do most people. I married straight out of college to a man who was three and a half years younger. Neither of us knew how to truly love another person. In our selfishness, we found many ways to hurt each other. As my husband developed relationships with other women, I felt betrayed and abandoned and resorted to the unhealthy coping strategies I had used in my youth. By the age of twenty-four, I filed for divorce and had an attention span of about thirty to sixty seconds. I covered it up at work, but the world kept moving while I was opting out. My greatest desire was to be put in a mental institution and left alone. I had reached the bottom of the barrel. My self-image felt like a ball of dirty, used bits of string held together with chewed chewing gum.

At that point, I cried out to God. "This is the best I could do, and this is it—string and gum! If you can do anything with this, do it. I'm done."

Soon after, I heard about a conference in Atlanta called the Basic Youth Conflicts Institute, offered by Bill Gothard. Several people from my church were going, so I joined them. We drove from Chattanooga to Atlanta and back each evening and stayed over Friday night for an all-day Saturday session. I had finally made space in my life for change to happen.

Throughout the conference, God seemed to hit me over the head every few minutes to get my attention. I learned many lessons, but the most valuable one was the importance of memorizing Scripture. Gothard, who had dyslexia as a child, began memorizing not verses or chapters, but whole books of the Bible. He believed God allowed his Word to heal his dyslexia. Gothard's goal was to memorize the entire Bible. As he said in the meeting, "Better to aim for the moon and get off the ground than to aim for a lightbulb and never get off the floor."

He challenged the audience—including me—that Scripture memory could heal minds negatively affected by drugs or alcohol. I didn't have those issues, but I had plenty of others! I began memorizing Psalm 131 that night and have continued memorizing Scripture to this day.

Interestingly, I got lost on the way to the place where I was spending the night. I used the verses I was memorizing to calm me down until my friends found me and showed me the way home.

LORD, my heart is not proud;
My eyes are not haughty.
I don't concern myself with matters too great
or too awesome for me to grasp.
Instead, I have calmed and quieted myself,
like a weaned child who no longer cries for its mother's milk.
Yes, like a weaned child is my soul within me.

O Israel, put your hope in the LORD—now and always. (Psalm 131)

The first book I memorized was James. It was both straightforward and challenging.

One thing I discovered about memorizing whole books of the Bible is that I couldn't skip the hard parts. If I chose verses to learn, I picked the ones I liked. But if you commit to learning it all, you must deal with some challenging words. For example, in Psalm 1, we might like verses 1-3, but then there are verses 4-6 that speak about the wicked as worthless chaff, being condemned at the judgment, and their path leading to destruction. But it is *all* God's Word, so we need to take note of all of it.

My strategy for memorizing is to read a verse several times each night before I sleep. Once I can say most of it correctly without looking, I add the next verse. That way, as I read the second verse, I'm also checking my accuracy on the first one. When the first two verses are done, I add the third—and so on. After about six verses, I pick up at verse seven and continue forward. Can I go back and quote the whole chapter? Sometimes. When I finish a chapter, I go on to the next one. Do I keep reviewing the ones I've learned? No. It's not a bad idea, but that isn't the point for me—my purpose is to meditate on them. *What is God saying to me through these words? Do I need to think differently? Do I need to change a behavior? Does my attitude please God? Is He warning me about something?*

I've often listened to someone sharing a problem, and verses come to mind that are relevant—either for them or for me. I can't always give the reference, but then numbers aren't my thing. Scripture memory hasn't helped my brain process numbers, but the Spirit recalls what I have stored in my heart (Psalm 119:11) and gives me perspective to share with someone else. When I need to make a decision, verses that guide me often come to mind.

After a few months, I started practicing my memory work while driving down the interstate to work—not the safest choice, but thankfully God protected me. One morning, I looked at the sun rising in the distance, and it was so beautiful, almost like driving into a picture. I said, "God, you did a great job on that sunrise this morning!"

And I felt him say, *Thank you. I made this one just for you.*

"Really?"

Yes. And I can make your life even more beautiful than this sunrise.

"You can?"

Yes.

"Then do it. Whatever it takes, do it."

And he has. My life has been far richer than I could have imagined. My dreams were so small. But God's plans were so big. I probably would have been terrified if I'd known what He had in store for me. But step by step, it has been a wonderful, fulfilling adventure.

Engaging with Scripture

1 Oh, the joys of those who do not follow the advice of the wicked, or stand around with sinners, or join in with mockers. 2 But
they delight in the law of the LORD, meditating on it day and
night. 3 They are like trees planted along the riverbank, bearing
fruit each season. Their leaves never wither, and they prosper in
all they do. 4 But not the wicked! They are like worthless chaff,
scattered by the wind. 5 They will be condemned at the time of
judgment. Sinners will have no place among the godly. 6 For the
LORD watches over the path of the godly, but the path of the
wicked leads to destruction. (Psalm 1)

Reflection Questions

- List the words in verses 1-3 that speak about those who follow God's directions.

- List words in verses 4-6 that describe "the wicked" or "sinners."

- Which of these descriptions do you want for yourself?

- Can you think of a time when a Scripture changed your way of thinking or acting? Describe what happened.

Scripture Meditation

You may use these scriptures to find wisdom for life and especially in hard times. As you read these Scriptures, you may find it helpful to use the *lectio divina* method mentioned in Chapter 2:

1. Read the passage, including as much context as you like.
2. Focus on the verses listed, and as you read them again, out loud if possible, listen for a word or phrase that calls to you. You may not know why—just listen for it.
3. Read the passage again and ask yourself, "Why this word? What is God saying to me?"
4. Finally, read the passage for the fourth time and just rest in the words God has for you today.

Day 1: **Deuteronomy 6:4-9** What recommendations do you find in these verses for staying close to the source of all wisdom?

Day 2: **Psalm 19** What are the sources of knowledge and wisdom shared here?

Day 3: **Psalm 119: 9-16** How can one stay pure?

____

____

Day 4: **Psalm 139** How well does God already know you?

____

____

____

____

____

Day 5: **Jeremiah 29:10-14** What is God's promise for hard times?

____

____

____

____

____

Day 6: **2 Corinthians 3:12-17** What is a Christian's purpose in life?

____

____

____

____

____

+ Scripture Memory

One important advantage of memorizing longer portions of Scripture is to protect us from taking verses out of context. One example I've heard goes like this: "Judas went out and hanged himself...Go and do likewise...and what thou doest, do quickly!" Of course, nothing in the Scriptures would ever suggest this scenario, but it shows the danger of focusing too much on just a phrase or two out of the context in which they were written.

As you consider Scripture memory to find space with God, try memorizing Psalm 1. Begin with one verse a day and add on as you go. While practicing this, notice how the scripture affects your daily life.

♫ Music Meditation

Songs can often help us remember. Choose one or two of the songs called "Psalm 1" from the playlist that resonates with you the most and listen to it several times this week.

? Reflections and Discussion

1. Leoma mentions how hard "adulting" is. Can you relate to the twenty-something-year-old man who told her, "You don't know what you can do until you get out there and find out."

   Recall some examples in your life when you had to get out there and do life. Were those times transitional or transformational? What did you learn from each, both good and bad?

   ____
   ____
   ____
   ____
   ____

2. "I cried out to God. 'This is the best I could do, and this is it—string and gum! If you can do anything with this, do it. I'm done.'"

   Have you ever felt like Leoma, like you were at the bottom of the barrel, and cried out to God? Did you feel God create an opening for you? What did it look like? How did you respond? Did you also open yourself to God?

   ____
   ____
   ____

3. "Interestingly I got lost on the way to the place where I was spending the night. I used the verses I was memorizing to calm me down until my friends found me and showed me the way home."

   Have you ever been afraid or distressed and had a verse or passage come to mind that comforted you or someone else? Have you sensed the Holy Spirit guiding you in a decision through scripture you have hidden in your heart?

4. How has God's grace made your life more beautiful than a sunrise? Ponder and journal about some transformative moments in your life.

5. Was there a spiritual practice, scripture meditation, or reflection in this chapter that felt particularly important or resonated with you? Why? How did it affect your daily experience and finding space with God?

CHAPTER 9

Finding a Sacred Community

These days, electronic communication is common. I've seen couples in restaurants, each of them glued to their phones. Were they texting each other—or someone else? They didn't seem to be present with the person they were with. As a result, loneliness has reached epidemic proportions. Where and when do you feel most alone? Why?

What is *community*? What does that word mean to you? According to Oxford Languages, community is:

1) a group of people living in the same place or having a particular characteristic in common.

2) a feeling of fellowship with others because of sharing common attitudes, interests, and goals.

We naturally seek out like-minded people. In school or college, we often form study groups or join those with the same interests in sports or activities. But when we enter the workforce, finding community becomes much more difficult.[32]

Clinical and community psychologist David McMillan defines community by four criteria:

> *...membership, influence, integration and fulfillment of needs, and shared emotional connection. To be part of a community, you must feel a sense of belonging (membership), feel like you make a difference to the group and that the group makes a difference to you (influence), feel like your needs will be met by other group members (integration and fulfillment of needs), and feel that you share*

history, similar experiences, time, and space together (shared emotional connection). [33]

Leoma's Story

In 2004, I felt God prompting me to leave my intense work in Africa to care for my eighty-five-year-old mother. It was an abrupt and difficult transition, but as I was the only child, it was the right decision. By that time, I had lived in Africa and England for twenty years. I had changed—and so had the culture at "home." When I moved back to the U.S. in May, I felt like a foreigner in my own country.

In Khartoum, I knew how things worked. I held a professorship at the University of Khartoum and acted as the linguistic coordinator for SIL in Sudan. But back in Tennessee, I felt insecure about even the basics. Card readers had come into use, and each one was different! At the doctor's office, after showing my insurance card, the receptionist asked, "Is there a co-pay on that?" I had no idea. What had happened to "my people"? What had happened to me?

During this confusing time, I met with the mission director at my church. As we talked, he asked what I missed the most.

"*Community,*" I said. In Sudan, I was surrounded by Sudanese and expatriates alike who knew me and understood my roles. Likewise, I knew them. We had many shared experiences and had mutual respect. In Tennessee, I felt like a stranger. No one really knew me. And other than caring for my mother, I didn't have a job. Who was I?

The mission director suggested I visit a group of women called the Order of St. Brigit in Knoxville—an ecumenical group of Christian women seeking to lead a more contemplative lifestyle. We formed a community without living together, as we were both single and married women. The support of that community has made an enormous difference in my life. It took time for me to feel confident that they would support me when I needed it, and that I would commit to the same for them. Trust takes time. Today, I'm blessed to be part of this very caring community.

Engaging with Scripture

[12] The human body has many parts, but the many parts make up one whole body. So, it is with the body of Christ. [13] Some of us are Jews, some are Gentiles, some are slaves, and some are free. But we have all been baptized into one body by one Spirit, and we all share the same Spirit. [14] Yes, the body has many different parts, not just one part. [15] If the foot says, "I am not a part of the body because I am not a hand," that does not make it any less a part of the body. [16] And if the ear says, "I am not part of the body because I am not an eye," would that make it any less a part of the body? [17] If the whole body were an eye, how would you hear? Or if your whole body were an ear, how would you smell anything? [18] But our bodies have many parts, and God has put each part just where he wants it. [19] How strange a body would be if it had only one part! [20] Yes, there are many parts, but only one body. [21] The eye can never say to the hand, "I don't need you." The head can't say to the feet, "I don't need you." [22] In fact, some parts of the body that seem weakest and least important are actually the most necessary. [23] And the parts we regard as less honorable are those we clothe with the greatest care. So we carefully protect those parts that should not be seen, [24] while the more honorable parts do not require this special care. So God has put the body together such that extra honor and care are given to those parts that have less dignity. [25] This makes for harmony among the members, so that all the members care for each other. [26] If one part suffers, all the parts suffer with it, and if one part is honored, all the parts are glad. (1 Corinthians 12:12-26)

Reflection Questions

The most important community we can be part of is "the body of Christ"—the church. So how do we become part of Christ's community, his body?

- Have you ever injured one part of your body? What became your most important body part?

- How does that fit with Paul's description here?

- How do these verses help you understand community?

- What about those members of the community who need more attention or care? Remember—all members of the community are broken in some way and will need healing and help at some point.

Scripture Meditation

These verses highlight the importance of belonging, fellowship, and mutual care in community.

Day 1: **Genesis 2:18-24** What was missing even before the Fall of man?

Day 2: **Ecclesiastes 4:7-12** What are the advantages of having others nearby?

Day 3: **1 Samuel 20:1-17** What is the value of a good friend?

Day 4: **Mark 1:16-20** How do you think the disciples benefited from their community?

Day 5: **Philippians 4:10-20** What did the support from the church in Philippi mean to Paul?

Day 6: **2 Corinthians 8:1-15** What is the advantage of being part of a larger community?

+ Spiritual Practices

The following practices will help you take practical steps toward building and nurturing sacred community in your own life.

1. OFFERING SPACE TO VISUALIZE COMMUNITY

An ancient prayer practice of the church is to experience God and transcendence by gazing at and reflecting upon icons. Henri Nouwen in *Behold the Beauty of the Lord* says, "...icons...are created for the sole purpose of offering access, through the gate of the visible, to the mystery of the invisible. Icons are created to bring us into the inner room of prayer and bring us close to the heart of God...they speak more to our inner than outer senses. An icon is like a window looking out upon eternity."[34]

I would like to introduce you to a famous icon known as *The Trinity* by Andrei Rublev.[35] As you prayerfully gaze upon it, ponder the importance of community and relationship within this Sacred Circle. Imagine yourself within the circle—notice that there is an opening at the front of the table just for you.

What might you want to say to the Father, the Son, and the Holy Spirit? What might they share with you? Take a moment to close your eyes and have a prayerful conversation with each member of the Trinity. Do you notice anything else in the icon that is drawing your attention? Journal your experience.

___

___

___

___

___

Originally this icon had a mirror in the bottom space at the table so those gazing into it could see themselves present at the table.

2. REFLECTIONS ABOUT COMMUNITY BY HENRI NOUWEN.

Nouwen lived part of his life in a community in France called L'Arche, where people—both with and without intellectual and physical challenges—live and work together. He found that living in a community was a rich and meaningful part of his life. Reflect on his quotes[36] below about community and highlight words or phrases that you resonate with. Ponder how Sacred Community might enrich your life.

> People who have known the joy of God point each other to flashes of light here and there and remind each other that they reveal the hidden but real Presence of God. They discover that there are people who heal each other's wounds, forgive each other's offenses, share their possessions, foster the spirit of community, celebrate the gifts they have received, and live in constant anticipation of the full manifestation of God's Glory.
>
> Henri Nouwen

> Community is first of all a quality of the heart. It grows from the spiritual knowledge that we are alive not for ourselves but for one another.
>
> Henri Nouwen[37]

> Solitude is very different from a 'time-out' from our busy lives. Solitude is the very ground from which community grows. Whenever we pray alone, study, read, write, or simply spend quiet time away from the places where we interact with each other directly, we are potentially opened for a deeper intimacy with each other.
>
> Henri Nouwen

> Jesus said Communion first, community comes out of that, and out of community, ministry.
>
> Henri Nouwen

> L'Arche is not a service institution or a group home. It is a community that exists to reveal God's love. Our people are given to the world to tell others about peace and forgiveness and celebration, to make them aware that in the midst of their brokenness, there is joy; in the midst of their wounded nature, there is healing.
>
> Henri Nouwen

> The best of community does give one a deep sense of belonging and well-being; and in that sense community takes away loneliness.
>
> Henri Nouwen

3. CREATING CONTEMPLATIVE COMMUNITY CONVERSATIONS

Henri Nouwen's ideal community was shaped out of a place of silence, contemplation, and presence. When each member of the community spends individual time on personal contemplative prayer practices, it naturally flows into a richer, fuller, more reflective space when the community comes together.

Leoma mentioned how much being a part of her contemplative community, the Order of Saint Brigit, has meant to her. I have also been a member of this community and various other contemplative communities, both in person and online, and I have truly flourished in these spaces.

If you don't currently belong to a contemplative community, consider creating one. Whether online or in person, a contemplative community "Offers Space for God's Presence" and usually includes time for silence, contemplative exercises or readings, and deep reflective conversation.

Here are a few guidelines for contemplative conversation and sharing within the space:

1. Use "I" statements when sharing from personal experiences or thoughts on the readings and reflections that connect with your everyday life.
2. Practice listening deeply - with the Holy Spirit, within yourself and to what others are saying. Listen with curiosity rather than judgment. This isn't a space for critiquing or fixing others in the group.
3. Notice common themes that arise during sharing.
4. Reflect before speaking and try to be concise.
5. Embrace and allow for times of silence within the conversation. Even if the silence is uncomfortable, resist the urge to fill it with words.
6. Try to avoid crosstalk.

♫ Music Meditation

Several songs are suggested as a possible way to continue your meditation as you go into the world including *Something Money Can't Buy*, *All Are Welcome in This Place*, and *Come To the Banquet Song* by Fay White. Listen to what speaks to you. Choose a song from the playlist that resonates with you the most and listen to it several times this week.

? Questions and Reflections for Journaling and Discussion

1. Where do you find community? Has it been difficult? Why?

   ____

   ____

   ____

   ____

   ____

2. What needs does a community provide for you?

____

____

____

____

____

3. As a member of a community, what is your role?

____

____

____

____

____

4. How can you contribute to helping the community grow and thrive?

____

____

____

____

____

5. One community you are likely part of is your work community. Do you think of your colleagues as your community? Why or why not?

____

____

____

____

____

6. How would your workplace change if you worked together as a community?

____

____

____

7. How about in a church or faith community? What connections have you found there?

As you reflect on your own experience, keep in mind the example of Jesus. Remember that even he chose to live in a community of disciples, and within that community, there were several smaller, more intimate communities.

8. Was there a spiritual practice, Scripture meditation, or reflection in this chapter that felt particularly important or resonated with you? Why? How did it affect your daily experience and your way of finding space with God?

CHAPTER 10

Becoming Wise: Looking to the Future

The journey of a thousand miles begins with a single step.
(Lao Tsu)

The way you walk now will determine who you will become in the years ahead. When you look back on your life, what do you hope to have accomplished? What kind of person do you want to be? Will you be proud of your choices or regret them?

Remember what we read in Chapter 4: The primary reason for examining your lifestyle and values...is to make sure that you are on the road you really want to travel.[38] Is that the road you're on now?

As the older generations pass away, they leave space for us to take up their mantles—to become the wise ones, the listeners, the questioners, the advisers. Trust me when I say that's an awesome responsibility.

Leoma's Story

When I started out as a missionary in my late twenties, I met an older missionary who had spent her adult life in a small village in Mexico, working on Bible translation. All she could talk about was what had happened there. She knew nothing outside of her little world—she had no idea who the President of the U.S. was, no clue about world events. I determined then and there that I was *not* going to end up like her.

The Internet didn't exist in 1982, so I purchased a shortwave radio and listened to it faithfully. I subscribed to a news magazine and read it. The Lord gave me opportunities to get to know people from a variety of countries, and I enjoyed learning about their languages and cultures. I wanted to become a "citizen of the world," and grow old with no regrets. If I hadn't done something, it would have been because I was busy with something I valued more. I wanted to live life to the fullest. Today, I'm seventy-five, and I believe I have accomplished my mission. But of course, there is still life to live, so I want to carry on to the end.

As I look back on my life, I'm amazed by where I've been and what I've done. My original goal was to be a speech therapist living in the southeastern United States. Instead, I've lived on three continents, completed a PhD, facilitated the translation of the Shilluk Bible by improving their writing system, and worked with thirty or more other languages in a similar way. In the final stage of my working life, I had the honor of directing training initiatives across sub-Saharan Africa. In my retirement, I've become an author and storyteller. And still I wonder—what's next?

But now let's turn our thoughts to what happens when those we care about die. When my father died of cancer, I was devastated. As far as I know, he was not a Christian. He and my mother had been married for fifty-one years, and her grief was beyond my comprehension. I knew I needed to care for her. Many people's life plans suddenly go sideways when a parent becomes ill or declines mentally. We owe a great debt to our parents for the care they gave us when we were helpless and dependent. Yet, they are not our children—they are our parents—and they deserve respect.

I was raised in a very loving home, but I realize others were not. For them, the decisions are perhaps harder. Should they show love to those who did not love them well? Does bad behavior excuse us from showing them love and care? What would Jesus do? What did Jesus do for you? Romans reminds us, "When you were yet sinners, Christ died for you." These are difficult questions to answer, but they are important ones to reflect on as you seek what God is asking of you.

When my mother transitioned to heaven at the age of ninety-two, I felt I had lost my confidant and closest friend. She had literally known me all my life. When I could no longer share my joys and sorrows with her, I wondered if life was even worth living. And then I realized what was wrong with that statement—I was now "the elder," and God was my go-to.

I never asked my mother what it felt like when her parents and siblings died, or how it felt to become the matriarch of our family. I wish I had. None of us in the next generation wants that role, but whether we accept it or not, we will get it. We will be the role models, the wise ones, the encouragers, the listeners, and the advisers. We've lived through many challenges and experiences, and it's now our turn to take up the mantle and share what we know with those facing the struggles of life. They may not always listen to us, but that's no excuse to stay silent. In time, the good advice we share will return to them and show them the way forward.

Engaging with Scripture

9 This is the account of Noah and his family. Noah was a righteous man, the only blameless person living on earth at the time,
and he walked in close fellowship with God. 10 Noah was the
father of three sons: Shem, Ham, and Japheth. 11 Now God saw
that the earth had become corrupt and was filled with violence.
12 God observed all this corruption in the world, for everyone on
earth was corrupt. 13 So God said to Noah, "I have decided to
destroy all living creatures, for they have filled the earth with violence. Yes, I will wipe them all out along with the earth! 14 "Build
a large boat from cypress wood and waterproof it with tar, inside
and out. Then construct decks and stalls throughout its interior.
15 Make the boat 450 feet long, 75 feet wide, and 45 feet high.

16 Leave an 18-inch opening below the roof all the way around the boat. Put the door on the side, and build three decks inside the boat—lower, middle, and upper. 17 "Look! I am about to cover the earth with a flood that will destroy every living thing that breathes. Everything on earth will die. 18 But I will confirm my covenant with you. So enter the boat—you and your wife and your sons and their wives. 19 Bring a pair of every kind of animal—a male and a female—into the boat with you to keep them alive during the flood. 20 Pairs of every kind of bird, and every kind of animal, and every kind of small animal that scurries along the ground, will come to you to be kept alive. 21 And be sure to take on board enough food for your family and for all the animals." 22 So Noah did everything exactly as God had commanded him. (Genesis 6:9-22)

We see more information from this passage in Matthew.

37 When the Son of Man returns, it will be like it was in Noah's day. 38 In those days before the flood, the people were enjoying banquets and parties and weddings right up to the time Noah entered his boat. 39 People didn't realize what was going to happen until the flood came and swept them all away. That is the way it will be when the Son of Man comes. (Matthew 24:37-39)

Reflection Questions

- What do you think the people thought about Noah and his action of building a boat?

- How did Noah respond to their mockery?

- What enabled Noah to complete the project God had given him?

- When God asks you to do something "odd," what is your response? Why?

- At the end of Noah's life, how did he view himself? How will you view yourself?

Scripture Meditation

LECTIO ON WISDOM SCRIPTURES

Spend some time meditating and praying about these scriptures. Ask the Holy Spirit how to apply this insight to your life. Journal what you notice.

Day 1: **Proverbs 2:1-15, Proverbs 13:20**

Day 2: **Matthew 7:21-26**

Day 3: **Proverbs 3:15, Proverbs 19:20**

Day 4: **James 1:5**

Day 5: **James 3:17**

____

____

____

____

____

Day 6: **Psalm 90:12**

____

____

____

____

____

+ Spiritual Practices

The above Scriptures call us to serve others as an expression of God's love. The practices that follow will help you consider concrete ways to live out that call in your daily life.

1. EXAMINING PAST CHOICES

Learning from our past decisions—both good and bad—can be an excellent way to grow in wisdom and help us make better choices in the future.

"In the movie *The Matrix,* Keanu Reeves plays Neo, an average man invited to see the radical truth of his world. In one scene, Neo rides in a car with a woman who already knows the truth about his world. Reluctant to accept her invitation to a new life, Neo opens the car door, ready to return to his former life. He peers down a dark, rainy street. The woman warns him not to choose that path.

When he asks why, she tells him, "Because you have been down there, Neo. You know that road. You know exactly where it ends. And I know that is not where you want to be." [39] (By the way, her name is Trinity.)

Practice: Recall a decision from your past—without judgment but with discernment—that ended up being a wrong choice. Trace the thoughts, feelings, influences, and circumstances that led up to the decision.

- What did you notice?
- Was there someone like Trinity advising you for or against a particular decision?
- Do you have a wise person you can consult when making important decisions?
- How could being aware of your thoughts and feelings help you avoid future mistakes?

Journal what you notice.

____

____

____

____

____

2. DEATHBED IMAGINATION EXERCISE

Think of an upcoming decision. Close your eyes and imagine yourself in the future on your deathbed. From that perspective, what advice would you give your current self? Also, imagine looking back on a life well lived. What would it look like? Journal what you notice.

> "And now the time is fast approaching for my release from this life, and I am ready to be offered as a sacrifice. I have fought the excellent fight. I have finished my full course with all my might, and I've kept my heart full of faith. There's a crown of righteousness waiting in heaven for me, and I know that my Lord will reward me on

his day of righteous judgment. And this crown is not only waiting for me, but for all who love and long for his unveiling." 2 Timothy 4: 6-8 (TPT)

"Tell me, what is it you plan to do with your one wild and precious life?" [40]

—Mary Oliver

___

___

___

___

___

3. INQUIRING OF GOD FOR WISDOM and GUIDANCE

As followers of Christ, inquiring of God should be natural when making life choices and big decisions—yet how often do we fail to pause, ask in prayer, and listen for guidance from the Holy Spirit?

Read this Old Testament example of David inquiring of the Lord for strategy:

> When the Philistines heard that David had been anointed king over Israel, all the Philistines went up in search of David; but David heard about it and went down to the stronghold. David inquired of the Lord, "Shall I go up against the Philistines? Will you give them into my hand?" The Lord said to David, "Go up; for I will certainly give the Philistines into your hand." So David came to Baal-perazim, and David defeated them there. He said, "The Lord has burst forth against my enemies before me, like a bursting flood." The Philistines abandoned their idols there, and David and his men carried them away.
>
> Once again, the Philistines came up and were spread out in the valley of Rephaim. When David inquired of the

> Lord, he said, "You shall not go up; go around to their rear and come upon them opposite the balsam trees. When you hear the sound of marching in the tops of the balsam trees, then be on the alert; for then the Lord has gone out before you to strike down the army of the Philistines. David did just as the Lord had commanded him; and he struck down the Philistines from Geba all the way to Gezer. (2 Samuel 5:17, 19-20a, 21-25, NRSV)

Even though we might not find ourselves in a situation like David's, life can throw us curveballs, causing us to make both immediate and long-term decisions. In those moments, there is wisdom in inquiring of the Holy Spirit, who is always available to guide us.

What do you notice in this passage?

David makes a similar inquiry both times—what were God's answers to each? Were they the same or different? How might this guide you when you face similar circumstances in your life?

During your prayer time this week, practice inquiring of God and then wait for the Spirit's still small voice. Try not to be discouraged if you don't receive an immediate answer—be aware of other ways God might guide you to answers during your days.

____

____

____

____

____

♫ Music Meditation

"*Build a Boat*" and "*Lead Me the Way*" are suggested as possible ways to continue your meditation as you go into the world. Listen to what speaks to you and listen to it several times this week.

? Questions and Reflections for Journaling and Discussion

1. When you reflect on the "elders" in your life, both wise and unwise, what lessons have you learned? Consider listening to a wise elder's story, both their triumphs and their difficulties.

____

____

____

____

____

2. And going back to the start of Chapter 10—when you grow old and look back on your life, what would give you the greatest sense of satisfaction that you have lived a good life?"

____

____

____

____

____

3. Was there a spiritual practice, scripture meditation, or reflection in this chapter that felt particularly important or resonated with you? Why? How did it affect your daily experience and finding space with God?

____

____

____

____

____

CHAPTER 11

Service: Reaching Out to Others

In figuring out your own life, complications arise. Maybe you get married and must adjust to the expectations of your spouse. You might have a child—and children have a way of taking over your life. You most likely have parents, and as they age, they will need help. As a family member, you have certain obligations to fulfill, and those can really upend the plans you made for yourself.

So, what should you do? Look out for "number one"? Or take a step back and offer your resources and abilities to help those in need? Either choice will cost you.

Leoma's Story

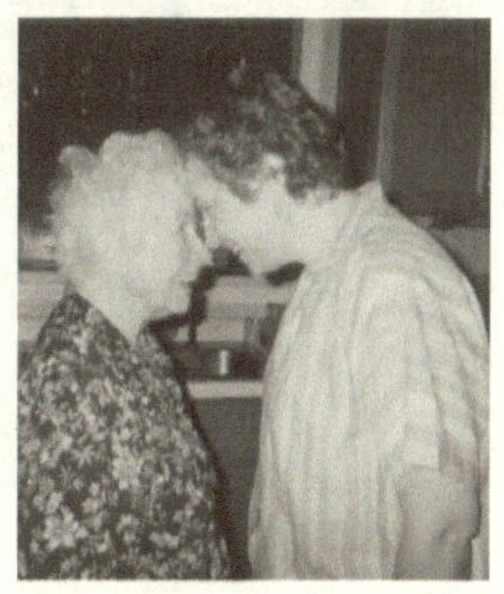

In May 2004, I left Khartoum and moved in with my mother in Knoxville, Tennessee. She had a marvelous sense of humor, and we enjoyed being together. This is one of my favorite photos (taken by Alison Crabb). Whenever we had a difference of opinion, I would use body language to assert my superiority. Mom would then say, "Get off my nose!"

I became Mom's caregiver, trying to balance respecting her as my mother with recognizing that not all her decisions were good for her. It is a tightrope to walk. Wherever we went, she was clearly the center of attention. As the family matriarch, everyone held her in high regard. I faded into the background, looking after her walker, making sure she had enough Kleenex, and clearing the path when she walked through a crowd. When she fell or had a medical issue, I stayed in the hospital with her, relieved at times by my cousins. My schedule revolved completely around her. That role continued for eight years, until she passed into heaven after a stroke.

While executing her estate, I realized I was now free to return to Africa. I had been the director of training for SIL in Africa from a distance, with many long-haul flights. Now I could live on the continent and go to the office. When I told my family of my plans, they asked, "Why?" My answer: "Because I can."

After another five years, I retired and moved back to the U.S. But I didn't return alone. A Rwandan colleague had six children, one of whom was a teenage boy who wanted to study in America.

I felt God calling me to host him. So, at sixty-six, I became the American "mom" to a sixteen-year-old named Ben. Not having children of my own, Ben was a learning experience. We discovered America together. I took him shopping and paid for his clothes. Teenagers eat—and my food bill went up. His shoes were scattered around the house, creating trip hazards. We worked on college applications. My learning curve was steep. He got on the high school soccer team, and I became a "grand-soccer-mom."

About the time he was accepted into the University of Tennessee, I received a payout from some investment my mom had made. The amount covered Ben's out-of-state tuition costs, and God made it very clear that my mom was providing a scholarship for Ben. He stayed with me through college and graduated as an engineer.

More recently, I met Sara and John[2*], who had come to the U.S. from South Sudan. A Sudanese American offered to marry Sara, so after a long process, she and John (a ten-year-old) came to Knoxville. Things went well for several years, but then Sara's husband began abusing Sara and her son. She attended my church, and a mutual friend introduced us. When I became aware of the difficulty of her situation, I felt God telling me to offer her my house while I was out of the country for a couple of months. She took me up on the offer and moved in during April 2024. When I returned home at the beginning of July, she still had nowhere to go. Her salary was too low to afford to pay for both rent and food, so she and John stayed with me until January 2025.

During that time, I read Henri Nouwen's definition of hospitality. "Hospitality is not to change people, but to offer them space where change can take place".[41] I learned through painful trial and error that I could not fix their situation. I put aside my writing and marketing to focus on helping them, but their problems were more complex than I could manage. God had to sort that out. My part was simply to offer space where change might happen. That I could do—though I had to remind myself often that my role was *not* to fix them but to offer space.

Why have I shared these stories? Because caring for others is costly—not just in terms of money, but also time, energy, and emotion. I learned humility in those days, whether with mom, Ben, or Sara and John. My purpose became helping others to succeed. Life was no longer about who I was, what I could do, or how important I was. My value was as a listener, adviser, confidant, and friend.

Would I do it again? In a heartbeat. Blessings don't flow just one way. I learned a great deal about loving others and about how God loves me during these training sessions. My focus is on heaven, not my possessions or privacy here on earth. The value of what I own is measured by how well I use it for the kingdom of God. Were

---

2 [*] Names have been changed to protect their privacy.

there painful times? Absolutely. Did I learn through them? Most certainly. Was it worth it? Yes—even though it was hard.

Are there people or places in your life where you might offer space for change to happen?

Engaging with Scripture

2 One day Ruth the Moabite said to Naomi, "Let me go out
into the harvest fields to pick up the stalks of grain left behind
by anyone who is kind enough to let me do it." Naomi replied,
"All right, my daughter, go ahead." 3 So Ruth went out to gather grain behind the harvesters. And as it happened, she found
herself working in a field that belonged to Boaz, the relative of
her father-in-law, Elimelech. 4 While she was there, Boaz arrived
from Bethlehem and greeted the harvesters. "The LORD be with
you!" he said. "The LORD bless you!" the harvesters replied. 5
Then Boaz asked his foreman, "Who is that young woman over
there? Who does she belong to?" 6 And the foreman replied, "She
is the young woman from Moab who came back with Naomi. 7
She asked me this morning if she could gather grain behind the
harvesters. She has been hard at work ever since, except for a few
minutes' rest in the shelter." 8 Boaz went over and said to Ruth,
"Listen, my daughter. Stay right here with us when you gather
grain; don't go to any other fields. Stay right behind the young
women working in my field. 9 See which part of the field they are
harvesting and then follow them. I have warned the young men
not to treat you roughly. And when you are thirsty, help yourself
to the water they have drawn from the well." 10 Ruth fell at his
feet and thanked him warmly. "What have I done to deserve such
kindness?" she asked. "I am only a foreigner." 11 "Yes, I know,"
Boaz replied. "But I also know about everything you have done
for your mother-in-law since the death of your husband. I have
heard how you left your father and mother and your own land
to live here among complete strangers. 12 May the LORD, the

God of Israel, under whose wings you have come to take refuge, reward you fully for what you have done." (Ruth 2:2-12)

Reflection Questions

- In what ways did Boaz offer care and hospitality to Ruth the Moabite here?

- Consider what ways Ruth and her mother-in-law Naomi showed care and hospitality toward one another.

- Are there places or people in your life that need space for change to happen?

- Could the space provided be physical, emotional, spiritual, or a combination?

Scripture Meditation

Consider these verses about service. Did those who served find it easy? Was it worthwhile? What effect did it have on those served?

Day 1: **John 13:1-17** How did Jesus serve the disciples?

Day 2: **Genesis 40** Does service always lead to a good outcome?

Day 3: **Romans 8:1-4** How has God served us?

Day 4: **Nehemiah 5:14-19** Who did Nehemiah depend on to reward his service?

Day 5: **Esther 2:21-23, 5:12 – 6:12** How did pride ruin Haman?

Day 6: **Isaiah 42:10-13** How is praise a service?

+ Spiritual Practices

The verses above highlight God's wisdom. The following practices will help you grow habits that will lead to a life of wisdom and maturity.

1. IMAGINATION EXERCISE

Pray that the Holy Spirit helps you experience the following Scripture through your imagination. Begin by reading the passage slowly several times. Then imagine yourself in the story—both as one of the characters and as an observer of the scene. Consider repeating this exercise several times during the week, choosing a different character each day. Your passage is Luke 10:25-37. Use verses 30-36 to imagine yourself in the parable. Journal your experience.

- Was there a character you related to most?

- Has there been a time in your life when you could relate to this story or a character in it?

  ____
  ____
  ____
  ____
  ____

- What did you learn from this exercise?

  ____
  ____
  ____
  ____
  ____

- Each time you finish, allow yourself to receive and be embraced in God's deep love for you. Carry this love and compassion with you into your day.

  ____
  ____
  ____
  ____
  ____

2. LECTIO ON A HOSPITALITY QUOTE

Read the following quote on hospitality slowly, three or four times, allowing space for stillness between each reading. Look for a word or phrase that stands out to you and take this into meditation and reflection. Have a conversation with God about this. Rest in God's presence. Journal your experience.

"Hospitality means primarily the creation of free space where the stranger can enter and become a friend instead of an enemy. Hospitality is not to change people, but to offer them space where change can take place." [42]

– Henri Nouwen

♫ Music Meditation

The songs *Scars*, *They'll Know We Are Christians (By Our Love)*, and *No Man Is an Island* are suggested as possible ways to continue your meditation as you go into the world. Listen to what speaks to you. Choose a song that resonates with you the most and listen to it several times this week.

? Questions and Reflections for Journaling and Discussion

1. Have there been situations or experiences in your life where you have received hospitality from another? What was that like?

2. Have there been times when you have offered hospitality to another? What was your experience? Was it difficult? If so, how? Were there gifts in it for you?

3. Was there a spiritual practice, scripture, meditation, or reflection in this chapter that felt particularly important or resonated with you? Why? How did it affect your daily experience and finding space with God?

____

____

____

____

____

CHAPTER 12

A Framework for Transformation

Congratulations on your having made it this far. Well done! But you may wonder, "How do I do all these things I've just learned?" The answer to that question is what this chapter is all about. So, let's get started.

Leoma's Story

Most jobs set the structure for your day. You need to arrive at work by a certain time, and your supervisor gives you the work you need to complete. Break times are scheduled, and when the designated hour comes, you can go home.

As an author, however, I have no boss and no set place I must be by a certain time. I can easily fritter away my mornings and afternoons and get nothing done. Stacy Ennis [43] explains that the brain needs a rhythm to spark creativity. One needs to develop a habit, a routine. As you follow that routine, the brain comes to know that at a certain point, it's time to be creative—it's time to write! She advocates fighting like a mama bear to protect that creative time—no appointments, no emails, no texts, no phone calls, no news, no social media. Even if you can squeeze in only fifteen minutes, use that time. I have found this protocol very helpful, and it's the reason this book is getting written. I've also found it helpful to set aside a consistent time to find space with God.

With my writing, I focus on content in the morning and take care of business, social media, and marketing in the afternoon.

For my time with God, I listen to Christian music during breakfast—the lyrics often remind me of God's character and give me the words to praise him. After breakfast, I move to a particular chair where God and I have time together. I've developed my own liturgy that includes worship, reading God's Word, confession, prayer, and committing myself into God's care for the day. I have another liturgy that I use before going to sleep, which includes reflection on my day and an Examen exercise.

To create a habit, we need a lot of repetition. It doesn't take much for us to fall out of a routine, so when it happens, we simply need to start again. Small steps may not seem like they're making a difference, but over time, they create big change. The good thing is that with God, we can start again anytime—even multiple times in a single day.

Our lives vary greatly, and what works for me may not work for you. You need to find your own rhythm. One thing I've learned is that God is a God of order, not of chaos. As we discover the best times and ways to meet with him, I believe he is always pleased to meet with us.

Engaging with Scripture

[18] "When he sits on the throne as king, he must copy for himself this body of instruction on a scroll in the presence of the
Levitical priests. [19] He must always keep that copy with him and
read it daily as long as he lives. That way he will learn to fear the
LORD his God by obeying all the terms of these instructions and
decrees. [20] This regular reading will prevent him from becoming proud and acting as if he is above his fellow citizens. It will
also prevent him from turning away from these commands in the
smallest way. And it will ensure that he and his descendants will
reign for many generations in Israel." (Deuteronomy 17:18-20)

Reflection Questions

- What were the two instructions given to the kings of Israel, and why were they important?

  ____
  ____
  ____
  ____
  ____

- Do you think all the kings followed these commands? Why or why not?

  ____
  ____
  ____
  ____
  ____

- What were the results when the commands were followed—and when they were not?

  ____
  ____
  ____
  ____
  ____

- What lessons can we learn for our own lives from their example?

  ____
  ____
  ____
  ____
  ____

Scripture Meditation

What do we learn about regular spiritual practices from these examples?

Day 1: **1 Corinthians 14:26-33** How does this passage express God's view of doing whatever you feel like, whenever you want to?

Day 2: **Exodus 29:38-46** What does this passage teach about planning and routine?

Day 3: **Proverbs 22:17-21** How do we gain wisdom?

Day 4: **Job 1:1-5** How did Job gain his reputation for being blameless and a man of complete integrity?

Day 5: **1 Corinthians 11:23-32** Why do we need to take our spiritual life seriously?

____

____

____

____

____

Day 6: **Proverbs 3:1-6** How do you store God's commands in your heart?

____

____

____

____

____

Writing a Rule of Life

What is a Rule of Life? It's not a legalistic rule, but a realistic rhythm—a structure for transformation through spiritual and life practices with the help of the Holy Spirit. Imagine yourself as a beautiful flowering vine that needs the support of a trellis to grow and flourish. This trellis represents your Rule of Life.

The term *Rule of Life* originated long ago within monasteries, where it provided a balanced daily rhythm and order for the community. An ancient rule still in use today in monasteries is the Rule of St. Benedict. St. Benedict's Rule created a balanced, focused and simple rhythm for the day including prayer, community, work, and rest/recreation. Even though we may not be monks living in monasteries, we still need intentional structures and rhythms for our lives to grow in our relationship with God and with one another. Without them, our lives can easily lose focus, priority, and peace, becoming a chaotic jumble.

As you reflect on these Scriptures, notice how they emphasize order, devotion, and intentional living. One way to live this out today is by creating a Rule of Life—a practical structure that supports your spiritual growth.

Consider setting aside uninterrupted blocks of time, or even a day or weekend retreat, to pray about and create your Rule of Life. This is the last chapter of our journey together—but your life journey continues. Creating your own Rule of Life will help you grow and flourish. Take your time with this. You may not complete your Rule in one week.

As a spiritual director, I have met with many people to review and consult on their personal Rules. Everyone is unique, and in different places on their spiritual journeys. When creating your Rule of Life, you may want to prayerfully consider the following questions:

1. What are my current God given desires, priorities, and gifts?

   ____
   ____
   ____
   ____
   ____

2. Where is God inviting me to grow?

   ____
   ____
   ____
   ____
   ____

3. What are my limitations, responsibilities, and obligations?

   ____
   ____
   ____
   ____
   ____

4. Where do I need balance in my life?

____

____

____

____

____

5. What spiritual practices do I feel drawn to include in my schedule?

____

____

____

____

____

6. Are there practices that would stretch me and help me grow?

____

____

____

____

____

7. Am I sensing my divine calling or purpose?

____

____

____

____

____

8. How can I simplify my life? Are there commitments that need to be eliminated or adjusted?

____

____

____

____

____

9. Is there a word, phrase, or Scripture verse that the Holy Spirit is highlighting for me to incorporate this year in my Rule of Life?

   ____

   ____

   ____

   ____

   ____

Once you have taken these questions to prayer, you can begin writing your "Rule of Life" for the year.

- You might start by writing your word, phrase, or scripture verse at the top of the page as a guiding theme.
- Next, consider some basic areas of life where you'd like to flourish—spiritual life and practices, physical well-being, relationships, play and rest, work/calling or service, and finances/giving. Focusing first on your spiritual life can help bring balance and focus to the other areas.

  "But seek first the kingdom of God and his righteousness, and all these things will be added to you." (Matthew 6:33, ESV)
- A good way to organize your Rule is by creating a box chart with your areas of life as headings across the top along with time frames in the side margin—Daily, Weekly, Monthly, Quarterly, and Yearly. Here is a possible example:

Daily	Bible reading	Prayer	Journaling	Diet and Exercise
Weekly	Church attendance	Small Group or Prayer Partner	Leisure/Sabbath	
Monthly	Giving	Spiritual Direction	Special Service	
Quarterly	Evaluate my Rule	Half or Day Retreat		
Yearly	Long Retreat	Plan and Review your Rule		

- If you choose not to use a chart, you can simply write your practices and goals on paper with the same time frames as headings.
- It's a good idea to incorporate your Rule of Life into your calendar or planner. If we don't connect our Rule with our calendar, the world and other people can overtake our schedules. Your Rule and calendar together can be a sacred structure against chaos. Start by looking at your current calendar. What are the needed adjustments? Notice when you feel energized or drained and plan your days accordingly.
- Review your Rule and calendar seasonally, pondering how you're doing and whether there are adjustments or updates needed. I've found it helpful to use a planner with a monthly view to see my rhythms at a glance.
- Ask yourself what challenges may make your Rule difficult? How will you hold yourself accountable? Try reviewing it with a trusted friend or spiritual director. Remember, our Rules and calendars don't have to be rigid. Allow for flexibility and God's grace.

"Teach us to number our days aright, that we may gain a heart of wisdom." (Psalm 90:12, NIV)

♫ Music Meditation

The Blessing and *These Times* are suggested as a possible way to continue your meditation as you go into the world. Listen to what speaks to you. Choose a song from the playlist that resonates with you the most and listen to it several times this week.

? Questions and Reflections for Journaling and Discussion

1. In reflecting on your journey through *Come, Find Space with God,* what stories and spiritual practices especially resonated with you?

   ____

   ____

   ____

   ____

   ____

2. What practices and rhythms do you sense the Holy Spirit inviting you into at this season of your journey?

   ____

   ____

   ____

   ____

   ____

3. What might challenge or block you from implementing these transformational practices and rhythms? What support might you need?

   ____

   ____

   ____

As you journey forward, Leoma and I pray abundant blessings upon you!

Irish Blessing

May the road rise to meet you;
may the wind be always at your back.
May the sun shine warm upon your face
and the rain fall softly on your fields.
Until we meet again,
may God hold you in the hollow of His hand.[44]

If you have found *Come, Find Space with God* helpful, please consider leaving a review on Amazon or Goodreads. Thank you so much.

Guidelines for Group Facilitators

Introduction

Leoma and I have been so richly blessed by the spiritual and faith communities and groups we have been a part of. We want to welcome you into this journey together for the next 12-13 weeks and beyond. We have been part of communities where there have been one or two facilitators or those where members take turns leading. You are free to choose what works best for your group.

Come, Find Space with God is designed for transformation rather than information, so we invite you into Sacred Community and Contemplative Conversation during your group time.

Following are suggested guidelines for your time together. Times are suggestions to make sure you get through the most important materials.

(First meeting)

Opening- Prayer and Brief Introductions and have each person write on a PostIt note what s/he hopes to take away from their time with *Come, Find Space with God.* You may want to collect these to reconsider at the end of the book.

You may choose to have a shorter first gathering by simply reviewing the Introduction of the book and open a discussion on *Life Stages* and *the Life of Faith Stages.* It is important for each person to consider where they are in these two journeys.

If you combine the Introduction and Chapter 1, you will need a longer time for the group to review their experiences with the reflections, practices and discussion questions. (See Chapter 9 on

Contemplative Conversation and perhaps review this prior to group sharing.)

Close- Prayer

Regular meetings

Opening-Prayer and reflect on the previous week's lesson. 10 minutes

Introduce the questions at the beginning of the new chapter and allow for brief discussion. 5 minutes

Read the story. One person could read the entire story, or several could read shorter portions of the story. This can be optional. 3-5 minutes

Read the Engaging with Scripture passage and discuss the reflection questions. 10 minutes

The Scripture Meditations are for use during daily devotions at home. Use the questions to guide your meditation.

Go to the Spiritual Practices and read through these answering any questions participants may have or guide participants through a practice together. Also, the Questions and Discussion topics can be completed through the week. 10 minutes or more as time allows

Close with prayer.

(If time allows you may want to adjust the time frames longer for some portions of the meeting to allow adequate space for reflection and sharing.)

References

Allen, Joseph J. Inner Way Toward a Rebirth of Eastern Christian Spiritual Direction. Holy Cross Orthodox Press, 2005.

Benner, David, and Larry Crabb. Sacred Companions: The Gift of Spiritual Friendship & Direction. InterVarsity Press, 2004.

Boyd, Gregory A. Seeing Is Believing, Experience Jesus Through Imaginative Prayer. Baker Books, 2004.

Calhoun, Adele Ahiberg. Spiritual Disciplines Handbook: Practices That Transform Us (Transforming Resources). InterVarsity Press, 2015.

Cassian, John. The Conferences by John Cassian. The First Conference: On the Goal of the Monk. Translated by Boniface Ramsey. XVII.I-III.I. Aeterna Press, 2015.

Cherry, Kendra. "Erikson's Stages of Development." Verywellmind, May 2, 2024. https://www.verywellmind.com/erik-eriksons-stages-of-psychosocial-development-2795740.

Clinebill, Howard. Growth Counseling for Mid-Years Couples. Fortress Press, 1977.

Comer, John Mark. Practicing the Way: Be with Jesus. Become like Him. Do as He Did. Practicing the Way. Random House Audio, 2024. Digital, 6 hours and 24 minutes.

Eagle, Ruth. What Does Kosher Mean? Medical News Today, 2024. https://www.medicalnewstoday.com/articles/what-is-kosher.

Ennis, Stacy. "How to Quadruple Your Writing Productivity and Get into Flow Faster." Paper presented at WIP Summit 2025. Women in Publishing

Summit, March 6, 2025.

Fleming, David L., S.J. Draw Me into Your Friendship: The Spiritual Exercises-A Literal Translation and a Contemporary Reading. Institute of Jesuit Sources, 1996.

Foster, Richard. Prayer: Finding the Heart's True Home. HarperOne, 2002.

Foster, Richard. Prayer: Finding the Heart's True Home. 2nd ed. HarperOne, 2009.

Foster, Richard, and Julia Roller, eds. A Year with God: Living Out the Spiritual Disciplines. HarperOne, 2009.

Giglio, Louie. "AZQuotes." n.d. Accessed November 18, 2025. https://www.azquotes.com/author/22501-Louie_Giglio.

Greig, Pete. How to Pray, A Simple Guide for Normal People. Christianaudio.com, 2019.

Haase, Albert. Coming Home to Your True Self: Leaving the Emptiness of False Attractions. InterVarsity Press, 2010.

Hagberg, Janet O., and Robert A. Guelich. THE CRITICAL JOURNEY, Stages in the Life of Faith. Sheffield Publishing, 2005.

"Irish Blessing." n.d. Accessed August 28, 2025. https://www.google.com/search?q=irish+blessing&rlz=1C5CHFA_enUS1002US1002&oq=Irish+blessing&gs_lcrp=EgZjaHJvbWUqCQgAEEUYOxiPAjIJCAAQRRg7GI8CMgYIARBFGDkyBwgCEAAYgAQyBwgDEAAYgAQyBwgEEAAYgAQyBwgFEAAYgAQyBwgGEAAYgAQyBwgHEAAYgAQyBwgIEAAYgAQyBwgJEAAYgATSAQg1NzE3ajBqN6gCALACAA&sourceid=chrome&ie=UTF-8.

Lanzetta, Beverly. Foundations in Spiritual Direction: Sharing the Sacred Across Traditions. Blue Sapphire Books, 2019.

Martin, James. The Jesuit Guide to (Almost) Everything: A Spirituality for Real Life. HarperOne, 2010.

Merton, Thomas. Thoughts in Solitude. Farrar, Straus and Giroux, 1999.

Nouwen, Henri. Behold the Beauty of the Lord. Revised. Ave Maria Press, 2007.

Nouwen, Henri. Bread for the Journey: A Daybook of Wisdom and Faith. Harper Collins, 2009.

Nouwen, Henri. Reaching Out, The Three Movements of the Spiritual Life. Doubleday, 1986.

Nouwen, Henri. Spiritual Direction: Wisdom for the Long Walk of Faith. HarperOne, 2015.

Nouwen, Henri. "Top 25 Quotes by Henri Nousen." Wind and Fly LTD. AZQuotes.Com, 2025. https://www.azquotes.com/quote/1070484,.

O'Brien, Kevin. The Ignatian Adventure, Experiencing the Spiritual Exercises of St. Ignatius in Daily Life. Loyola Press, 2011.

Oliver, Mary. New and Selected Poems. One. Beacon Press, 2004.

Pickering, Sue. Spiritual Direction: A Practical Introduction. Hymns Ancient & Modern Ltd, 2008.

Rublev, Andrei. Trinity Icon. With hramikona. n.d. Digital file, 9.6"x16.1". https://www.etsy.com/listing/1783936881/the-holy-trinity-andrei-rublev-download?favorite_listing_id=1783936881.

Rupp, Joyce. Open the Door: A Journey to the True Self. Soren Books, 2008.

Salman, Warner. Jesus Knocking on the Door. n.d. Accessed August 26, 2025. https://i.pinimg.com/736x/39/0a/b2/390ab203a2f64c9fec4d97ff5a5e480a--my-grandmother-grandmothers.jpg.

Thibodeaux, Fr Mark. SJ. Armchair Mystic: How Contemplative Prayer Can Lead You Closer to God. Franciscan Media, 2019.

Thibodeaux, Fr Mark. SJ. God's Voice Within: The Ignatian Way to Discover God's Will. Loyola Press, 2010.

Volpe, Allie. "Why Community Matters so Much -- and How to Find Yours." Vox, Life / Even Better, March 24, 2022. https://www.vox.com/22992901/how-to-find-your-community-as-an-adult.

Endnotes

1 Henri Nouwen, *Reaching Out, The Three Movements of the Spiritual Life* (Doubleday, 1986).

2 Kendra Cherry, "Erikson's Stages of Development," *Verywellmind*, May 2, 2024, https://www.verywellmind.com/erik-eriksons-stages-of-psychosocial-development-2795740.

3 Janet O. Hagberg and Robert A. Guelich, *THE CRITICAL JOURNEY, Stages in the Life of Faith* (Sheffield Publishing, 2005).

4 Louie Giglio, "AZQuotes," n.d., accessed November 18, 2025, https://www.azquotes.com/author/22501-Louie_Giglio.

5 John Mark Comer, *Practicing the Way: Be with Jesus. Become like Him. Do as He Did.*, Practicing the Way, Random House Audio, 2024, Digital, 6 hours and 24 minutes.

6 Warner Salman, *Jesus Knocking on the Door*, n.d., accessed August 26, 2025, https://i.pinimg.com/736x/39/0a/b2/390ab203a2f64c9fec4d97f-f5a5e480a--my-grandmother-grandmothers.jpg.

7 Joyce Rupp, *Open the Door: A Journey to the True Self* (Soren Books, 2008), 13.

8 Gregory A. Boyd, *Seeing Is Believing, Experience Jesus Through Imaginative Prayer* (Baker Books, 2004), 12.

9 Kevin O'Brien, *The Ignatian Adventure, Experiencing the Spiritual Exercises of St. Ignatius in Daily Life* (Loyola Press, 2011).

10 Richard Foster and Julia Roller, eds., *A Year with God: Living Out the Spiritual Disciplines.* (HarperOne, 2009), xxviii.

11 Fr. Mark Thibodeaux, SJ, *Armchair Mystic: How Contemplative Prayer Can Lead You Closer to God* (Franciscan Media, 2019).

12 Adele Ahiberg Calhoun, *Spiritual Disciplines Handbook: Practices That Transform Us (Transforming Resources)* (InterVarsity Press, 2015).

13 Richard Foster, *Prayer: Finding the Heart's True Home* (HarperOne, 2002), 1–2.

14 Ruth Eagle, *What Does Kosher Mean?* (Medical News Today, 2024), https://www.medicalnewstoday.com/articles/what-is-kosher.

15 Howard Clinebill, *Growth Counseling for Mid-Years Couples* (Fortress Press, 1977).

16 Pete Greig, *How to Pray, A Simple Guide for Normal People*, christianaudio.com, 2019.

17 Richard Foster, *Prayer: Finding the Heart's True Home*, 2nd ed. (HarperOne, 2009).

18 Kevin O'Brien, *The Ignatian Adventure, Experiencing the Spiritual Exercises of St. Ignatius in Daily Life.*

19 James Martin, *The Jesuit Guide to (Almost) Everything: A Spirituality for Real Life* (HarperOne, 2010).

20 Albert Haase, *Coming Home to Your True Self: Leaving the Emptiness of False Attractions* (InterVarsity Press, 2010).

21 Albert Haase, *Coming Home to Your True Self: Leaving the Emptiness of False Attractions*, 122.

22 Pete Greig, *How to Pray, A Simple Guide for Normal People.*

23 Fr. Mark Thibodeaux, SJ, *God's Voice Within: The Ignatian Way to Discover God's Will* (Loyola Press, 2010), 218.

24 David L. Fleming S.J., *Draw "Me into Your Friendship: The Spiritual Exercises-A Literal Translation and a Contemporary Reading* (Institute of Jesuit Sources, 1996), SE 23.

25 Thomas Merton, *Thoughts in Solitude* (Farrar, Straus and Giroux, 1999).

26 David Benner and Larry Crabb, *Sacred Companions: The Gift of Spiritual Friendship & Direction* (InterVarsity Press, 2004), 94.

27 Sue Pickering, *Spiritual Direction: A Practical Introduction* (Hymns Ancient & Modern Ltd, 2008), 4.

28 Joseph J. Allen, *Inner Way Toward a Rebirth of Eastern Christian Spiritual Direction* (Holy Cross Orthodox Press, 2005), 5.

29 Henri Nouwen, *Spiritual Direction: Wisdom for the Long Walk of Faith* (HarperOne, 2015), 9.

30 Beverly Lanzetta, *Foundations in Spiritual Direction: Sharing the Sacred Across Traditions* (Blue Sapphire Books, 2019), 4.

31 John Cassian, *The Conferences by John Cassian. The First Conference: On the Goal of the Monk*, trans. Boniface Ramsey, XVII.I-III.I (Aeterna Press, 2015), 56–57.

32 *Oxford Languages*, "Community," https://www.google.com/search?q=community+meaning&rlz=1C5CHFA_enUS1002US1002&oq=community+mea&gs_lcrp=EgZjaHJvbWUqDwgBEAAYRhj5ARixAxiABDIGCAAQRRg5Mg8IARAAGEYY-QEYsQMYgAQyBwgCEAAYgAQy-

BwgDEAAYgAQyBwgEEAAYgAQyBwgFEAAYgAQyBwgGEAAY-gAQyBggHEEUYPNIBCTExOTIwajBqN6gCALACAA&sourceid=-chrome&ie=UTF-8.

33 Allie Volpe, "Why Community Matters so Much -- and How to Find Yours," *Vox*, Life / Even Better, March 24, 2022, 2, https://www.vox.com/22992901/how-to-find-your-community-as-an-adult.

34 Henri Nouwen, *Behold the Beauty of the Lord*, Revised (Ave Maria Press, 2007), 23.

35 Andrei Rublev, *Trinity Icon*, with hramikona, n.d., digital file, 9.6"x16.1", https://www.etsy.com/listing/1783936881/the-holy-trinity-andrei-rublev-download?favorite_listing_id=1783936881.

36 Henri Nouwen, "Top 25 Quotes by Henri Nousen," Wind and Fly LTD, AZQuotes.Com, 2025, https://www.azquotes.com/quote/1070484,.

37 Henri Nouwen, *Bread for the Journey: A Daybook of Wisdom and Faith* (Harper Collins, 2009), 23.

38 Howard Clinebill, *Growth Counseling for Mid-Years Couples*.

39 James Martin, *The Jesuit Guide to (Almost) Everything: A Spirituality for Real Life*, 337.

40 Mary Oliver, *New and Selected Poems*, One (Beacon Press, 2004).

41 Howard Clinebill, *Growth Counseling for Mid-Years Couples*.

42 Henri Nouwen, *Reaching Out, The Three Movements of the Spiritual Life*.

43 Stacy Ennis, "How to Quadruple Your Writing Productivity and Get into Flow Faster," paper presented at WIP Summit 2025, *Women in Publishing Summit*, March 6, 2025.

44 "Irish Blessing," n.d., accessed August 28, 2025, https://www.google.com/search?q=irish+blessing&rlz=1C5CHFA_enUS1002US1002&oq=Irish+blessing&gs_lcrp=EgZjaHJvbWUqCQgAEEUYOxiPAjIJCAAQRRg-7GI8CMgYIARBFGDkyBwgCEAAYgAQyBwgDEAAYgAQyBwgEEAAY-gAQyBwgFEAAYgAQyBwgGEAAYgAQyBwgHEAAYgAQyBwgIEAAY-gAQyBwgJEAAYgATSAQg1NzE3ajBqN6gCALACAA&sourceid=-chrome&ie=UTF-8.

www.ingramcontent.com/pod-product-compliance
Lightning Source LLC
LaVergne TN
LVHW090954080826
845145LV00003B/1009

* 9 7 8 0 9 7 9 8 9 6 6 8 2 *